P9-DMC-358

POLICY

The Reinterpretation

VERSUS

of the ABM Treaty

THE LAW

Raymond L. Garthoff

POLICY VERSUS THE LAW

RAYMOND L. GARTHOFF

POLICY VERSUS THE LAW

The Reinterpretation
of the ABM Treaty

THE BROOKINGS INSTITUTION
Washington, D.C.

WITHDRAWN

Tennessee Tecn. Library
Cookeville. Tenn.
388234

Copyright © 1987 by
THE BROOKINGS INSTITUTION
1775 Massachusetts Avenue, N.W., Washington, D.C. 20036

Library of Congress Catalog Card Number 87-72297

ISBN 0-8157-3049-7

9 8 7 6 5 4 3 2 1

Board of Trustees

Louis W. Cabot
Chairman
Ralph S. Saul
Vice Chairman;
Chairman, Executive Committee;
Chairman, Development Committee
Samuel H. Armacost
J. David Barnes
Rex J. Bates
A. W. Clausen
William T. Coleman, Jr.
Richard G. Darman
Thomas R. Donahue
Charles W. Duncan, Jr.
Walter Y. Elisha
Robert F. Erburu
Roberto C. Goizueta
Robert D. Haas
Philip M. Hawley
Roy M. Huffington
B. R. Inman
Vernon E. Jordan, Jr.
James A. Joseph
James T. Lynn
Donald F. McHenry
Bruce K. MacLaury
Mary Patterson McPherson
Maconda B. O'Connor
Donald S. Perkins
J. Woodward Redmond
James D. Robinson III
Robert V. Roosa
B. Francis Saul II
Henry B. Schacht
Howard R. Swearer
Morris Tanenbaum
James D. Wolfensohn
Ezra K. Zilkha
Charles J. Zwick

Honorary Trustees

Vincent M. Barnett, Jr.
Barton M. Biggs
Eugene R. Black
Robert D. Calkins
Edward W. Carter
Frank T. Cary
Lloyd N. Cutler
Bruce B. Dayton
Douglas Dillon
Huntington Harris
Andrew Heiskell
Roger W. Heyns
John E. Lockwood
William McC. Martin, Jr.
Robert S. McNamara
Arjay Miller
Charles W. Robinson
H. Chapman Rose
Gerard C. Smith
Robert Brookings Smith
Sydney Stein, Jr.
Phyllis A. Wallace

THE BROOKINGS INSTITUTION is an independent organization devoted to nonpartisan research, education, and publication in economics, government, foreign policy, and the social sciences generally. Its principal purposes are to aid in the development of sound public policies and to promote public understanding of issues of national importance.

The Institution was founded on December 8, 1927, to merge the activities of the Institute for Government Research, founded in 1916, the Institute of Economics, founded in 1922, and the Robert Brookings Graduate School of Economics and Government, founded in 1924.

The Board of Trustees is responsible for the general administration of the Institution, while the immediate direction of the policies, program, and staff is vested in the President, assisted by an advisory committee of the officers and staff. The by-laws of the Institution state: "It is the function of the Trustees to make possible the conduct of scientific research, and publication, under the most favorable conditions, and to safeguard the independence of the research staff in the pursuit of their studies and in the publication of the results of such studies. It is not a part of their function to determine, control, or influence the conduct of particular investigations or the conclusions reached."

The President bears final responsibility for the decision to publish a manuscript as a Brookings book. In reaching his judgment on the competence, accuracy, and objectivity of each study, the President is advised by the director of the appropriate research program and weighs the views of a panel of expert outside readers who report to him in confidence on the quality of the work. Publication of a work signifies that it is deemed a competent treatment worthy of public consideration but does not imply endorsement of conclusions or recommendations.

The Institution maintains its position of neutrality on issues of public policy in order to safeguard the intellectual freedom of the staff. Hence interpretations or conclusions in Brookings publications should be understood to be solely those of the authors and should not be attributed to the Institution, to its trustees, officers, or other staff members, or to the organizations that support its research.

Foreword

THE Iran-Contra dealings have focused attention on a case of conflict between what were perceived as policy imperatives and the law. While congressional hearings have drawn attention to that case, another of no less importance in political, international diplomatic, and constitutional terms has not been sufficiently understood. The Reagan administration's reinterpretation of the ABM Treaty to facilitate its Strategic Defense Initiative (SDI) program poses a comparable issue of policy versus the law.

The ABM Treaty, signed and ratified in 1972, bans the development and testing, as well as deployment, of space-based and other mobile ABM systems or system components. The reinterpretation, first advanced in 1985, maintains that because of the structure of the treaty and the record of its negotiation, this prohibition does not apply to systems based on new technologies. This study reviews that argument and rejects its validity.

The author, Raymond L. Garthoff, a senior fellow in the Brookings Foreign Policy Studies program since his retirement from government service in 1979, is in a unique position to provide an authoritative assessment of the issue. Ambassador Garthoff was one of the principal negotiators of the ABM Treaty and personally negotiated key provisions involved in the disputed interpretation. His analysis is based upon both a careful review of the record and his own recollections. It summarizes and documents the sequence of steps involved in reaching final agreement on the language of the treaty, as well as the intentions and perceptions of the negotiators as they conducted the process.

The analysis sets in context those official documents that have recently been declassified in support of the reinterpretation. It also notes and generally describes important steps in the negotiation whose documentation has not been declassified. In some instances, unclassified document reference numbers are provided for those who either immediately or in the future are in a position to compare Ambassador Garthoff's characterization with the official record.

The ABM Treaty reinterpretation poses profound questions as to the functioning of American political and governmental decisionmaking processes, and as to compliance with the law of the land and international obligations. It is clearly a matter that should receive the most careful scrutiny and public discussion.

The author wishes to acknowledge his appreciation for comments on the manuscript from Robert G. Bell, Lloyd N. Cutler, Sidney N. Graybeal, John B. Rhinelander, Gerard C. Smith, and John D. Steinbruner. He also wishes to thank Denise DiLima for typing the manuscript, Stephen K. Wegren and Kim Motylewski for verifying the published source references, and Jeanette Morrison and Brenda B. Szittya for editing the manuscript.

Brookings gratefully acknowledges the financial support for this book provided by the Andrew W. Mellon Foundation, the Carnegie Corporation of New York, and the John D. and Catherine T. MacArthur Foundation.

The views in this book are those of the author and should not be ascribed to the persons or foundations whose assistance is acknowledged, or to the trustees, officers, or other staff members of the Brookings Institution.

BRUCE K. MAC LAURY
President

August 1987
Washington, D.C.

Contents

I

The Issue

THE SECRET Iran-Contra arms deal violated the sensibility of the American people and Congress, and in at least some important particulars the law of the land. The American public has, however, had a natural tendency to see the affair as an aberration, even as it has gone from a question of poor judgment in the White House over dealings with the Khomeini regime and a puzzling diversion of weapon-sale "profits," to flagrant violations of the law by White House and Central Intelligence Agency officials in providing arms to the Contras through a mysterious pseudo-unofficial "Enterprise." Regrettably, these activities bear a close resemblance to another national security initiative that is potentially even more significant, the Reagan administration's attempt since 1985 to reinterpret the Antiballistic Missile Treaty of 1972.[1] At the core of both is a belief that the president of the United States, as the

1. The full formal title is "Treaty Between the United States of America and the Union of Soviet Socialist Republics on the Limitation of Anti-ballistic Missile Systems." The text and associated formal Agreed Statements of interpretation are given in the Appendix below, drawn from the Arms Control and Disarmament Agency, *Arms Control and Disarmament Agreements: Texts and Histories of Negotiations,* 1982 ed. (Washington, D.C.: ACDA, 1982), pp. 139–47.

executive authority, makes foreign policy and that his exercise of this power should not be trammeled by the legislative or judicial branches except in the most narrow explicit constraints on use of the public treasury. Both are cases of conflicts between perceived policy imperatives and the law. Compounding and confusing the issue, haphazard decisionmaking and recurrent disorder have also characterized these activities.

Signed by President Richard M. Nixon on May 26, 1972, in Moscow, the ABM Treaty was ratified after advice and consent by a vote of 88-2 of the U.S. Senate and entered into force on October 3, 1972. It is a treaty of unlimited duration. It is of course subject to amendment, withdrawal, or termination by the two parties, either under its own specified terms or in accordance with the general international practice and law of treaties. By the same token, however, it is not open to material *unilateral* revision.

President Ronald Reagan has claimed that for the thirteen years from 1972 until 1985 the Nixon, Ford, and Carter administrations (and his own) labored under a misimpression as to the actual obligation of the ABM Treaty.

The immediate issue is whether that claim is justified. The larger question, as in the case of the Iran-Contra affair, is how far the U.S. government should go in supporting the policies of a president when those policies are constrained or frustrated by observance of the law of the land. In the case of the ABM Treaty, the issue also involves the international obligations and the international standing of the United States.

Origins of the Reinterpretation

On October 6, 1985, the then national security adviser, Robert C. McFarlane, during an appearance on "Meet the Press," casually indicated that the Reagan administration had redefined a key obligation of the ABM Treaty. McFarlane did not announce that the administration had reexamined the record and reinterpreted the obligations of the treaty. He simply gratuitously declared, in response to a question that had not even mentioned the ABM Treaty, that testing and development of ABM systems based on "new physical concepts" was "approved and authorized by the [ABM] treaty."[2] The reinterpretation was thus first made public through the unorthodox procedure of referring to it on a national television program.

Even Secretary of State George P. Shultz was caught by surprise by this public announcement, unaware that any decision had been made on the matter, one on which the secretary had substantial reservations that he had never had the opportunity to raise with the president. In fact, there is no indication that McFarlane had even discussed the matter with the president before he spoke publicly. When a White House spokesman confirmed at a press briefing two days later that this new interpretation was official, the significance of the issue became apparent. There was an immediate alarm from several quarters in the United States and from the NATO allies, who had not been consulted or even informed about this important change affecting the key agreement underpinning East-West arms control and, in the view of many, strategic stability. Both Prime Minister Margaret Thatcher of Great Britain and Chancellor Helmut Kohl of West Germany promptly wrote to President Reagan questioning the action. It was a repeat of the reaction to the president's "Star Wars" speech of March 1983 launching the Strategic Defense Initiative. But this time there was not even a presidential announcement, and rather than tentatively chart a new course for the future, the new initiative purported to reinterpret the past and threatened to upset the present.

Three days later, on October 11, President Reagan finally met on the issue for the first time with Secretary of State Shultz, Secretary of Defense Caspar W. Weinberger, Arms Control and Disarmament Agency Director Kenneth L. Adelman, and McFarlane. After an evidently acrimonious argument, with Shultz opposing the reinterpretation and Weinberger championing it, a

2. See "Mr. McFarlane's Interview on 'Meet the Press,' " October 6, 1985, in *Department of State Bulletin*, vol. 85 (December 1985), p. 33. (Hereafter cited as *State Bulletin*.)

bureaucratic compromise was fashioned and codified the next day in National Security Decision Directive (NSDD)–192.[3] Reportedly, apart from the strong policy advocacy of Weinberger, the president finally decided not to repudiate the reinterpretation because to admit such a pronouncement had been made prematurely would not reflect well on McFarlane and the administration.

The new compromise position was disclosed by Secretary Shultz two days later in a speech to the North Atlantic Assembly. On the one hand, it was claimed that the new, "broader interpretation" was "based on a careful analysis of the treaty text and the negotiating record" and "fully justified." On the other hand, it was declared "a moot point," because the administration would continue to conduct its SDI program "in accordance with a restrictive interpretation of the treaty's obligations" such as had prevailed since 1972.[4]

In fact, this compromise position by no means made the matter "a moot point" except in the very limited sense of quieting current political controversy in Washington and with the NATO allies. On the contrary, the administration had affirmed the validity of the reinterpretation and had asserted its option to change the basis for its own SDI program at any time of its choice. In effect it had also declared that the Soviet Union would be justified in acting at its pleasure on the basis of the broader interpretation. Thus, while the outcome of the belated high-level review was a compromise, it was one that did not settle the underlying issue.

What is the new interpretation? Article V(1) of the ABM Treaty states: "Each Party undertakes not to develop, test, or deploy ABM systems or components which are sea-based, air-based, space-based, or mobile land-based." The new, broader interpretation holds that under the treaty the parties *are* allowed to develop and test ABM systems and components that are sea-based, air-

---

3. The fullest and best-informed account is Don Oberdorfer, "ABM Reinterpretation: A Quick Study," *Washington Post,* October 22, 1985. He did not, however, identify the NSDD, which I learned about from other sources.

4. "Arms Control, Strategic Stability, and Global Security: Secretary Shultz's Address before the North Atlantic Assembly in San Francisco on October 14, 1985," *State Bulletin,* vol. 85 (December 1985), p. 23.

based, space-based, and mobile land-based—if they are based on new physical principles (such as lasers or particle beams). The administration's claim rests on a complex chain of argument, because of the effects of a number of interrelated provisions of the treaty. The key element is that systems based on "other physical principles" are not explicitly mentioned in Article V(1), or indeed anywhere in the body of the treaty itself, but only in associated Agreed Interpretation D, which relates solely to deployment and not to development and testing. Supporters of the reinterpretation contend that because the body of the treaty itself nowhere explicitly deals with future ABM systems, the treaty permits them except as constrained by Agreed Statement D. The logic of the interrelation of the various elements of the treaty, and the negotiating record, must be reviewed in detail in order to establish, or to refute, this claim.

If valid, the new, broader interpretation would open up much greater opportunities for development and testing under the administration's Strategic Defense Initiative (SDI). And the new interpretation, indeed, emerged from an intensive effort in the Office of the Secretary of Defense to find greater leeway for the SDI. As Lieutenant General James A. Abrahamson, USAF, the director of the Strategic Defense Initiative Organization, testified before Congress: "There clearly will come a time when we enter the development phase—and the development phase will require [so] much more direct testing, that we will have to have a modified treaty *in some way* in order to proceed. . . ."[5] Without doubt unilaterally reinterpreting the treaty in a permissive direction was the easiest way to modify it. Amending it would require concurrence not only of the U.S. Senate but also of the Soviet Union. Withdrawing from it would entail a major political battle in the United States, as well as serious negative political repercussions in the NATO alliance and in relations with the Soviet Union, including almost certainly a sharp break in the process of U.S.-Soviet arms control across the board.

5. *Strategic Defense Initiative*, Hearings before the Subcommittee on Strategic and Theater Nuclear Forces of the Senate Armed Services Committee, 99 Cong. 1 sess. (Government Printing Office, 1986), p. 40; emphasis added.

The idea that the ABM Treaty did not mean what it plainly seemed to say, and what everyone had believed it to say for years, had originated with the late Donald G. Brennan at the Hudson Institute in 1975, and independently with Abraham S. Becker and William R. Harris at the Rand Corporation in 1977; it was publicly surfaced by the Heritage Foundation in April 1985.[6] It emerged in

6. T. K. Jones, in the Office of the Secretary of Defense, in late 1984 and early 1985 commissioned studies to review the ABM Treaty and its negotiating history to see if there were any loopholes that would allow more leeway for the SDI program, and to ascertain whether the United States was holding itself to a more narrow interpretation than the Soviet Union. One of these papers, requested of William R. Harris of the Rand Corporation on January 23, 1985, was submitted in only two weeks, on February 7. As Jones knew when he requested the memorandum, Harris's approach opened the door to a possible broad reinterpretation based simply on his dissection of the logic of the construction of the treaty and a selective use of the ratification record—an approach Harris had been pushing for seven years. A more thorough study, however, based on the classified negotiating record and prepared by former negotiators Colonel Charles L. Fitzgerald and Sidney N. Graybeal of the Systems Planning Corporation, was submitted in March. That study, in effect, reaffirmed the traditional interpretation. Then, on April 4, crediting an anonymous government official, the Heritage Foundation issued a backgrounder proposing a version of the broad interpretation and titled *U.S.-Soviet Arms Accords Are No Bar to Reagan's Strategic Defense Initiative,* Heritage Foundation Backgrounder 421 (Washington, D.C., April 1985).

The idea behind the broad interpretation had been raised by Brennan and Becker in a round of correspondence in 1977. It was quashed at that time partly as a result of an exchange of Letters to the Editor in *International Security* (vol. 2 [Summer 1977], pp. 106–09) between Mr. Becker and myself, and partly as the result of a round-robin correspondence between Becker, Brennan, Gerard C. Smith, John B. Rhinelander, Herbert Scoville, Jr., Paul H. Nitze, and myself. Brennan ended that exchange by capitulating. In a letter to Rhinelander on July 15, 1977, Brennan said: "In the face of this level of analysis [in Rhinelander's letter, which Brennan also called "detailed, persuasive and definitive"], not to mention the essential concurrence of Smith, Nitze, and Garthoff, any further insistence that the Treaty does not necessarily ban the development of (among others) space-based exotic ABM systems would have to be reckoned willful, indeed obstinate, stupidity." (Quoted by permission.) Coming from an ardent progenitor of strategic defenses, this can be read as a perceptive epitaph for the reinterpretation years in advance! Harris, however, persisted in holding to his view.

Harris had a new chance in the Reagan administration. In early 1981 the transition team in charge of the Arms Control and Disarmament Agency, Michael E. Pillsbury and David S. Sullivan, hired Harris as a consultant to help prepare a study of Soviet arms control violations. In the course of this work on ABM Treaty compliance, Harris, known to Pillsbury from earlier service together at

the U.S. government in September 1985 as the result of a review prepared by a young former New York assistant attorney general, Philip H. Kunsberg, for the Office of the Secretary of Defense. Kunsberg had been asked by Richard N. Perle, the assistant secretary of defense for international security, and Fred C. Iklé, undersecretary of defense for policy, in the spring of 1985 to take a fresh look and see if there was more leeway in the ABM Treaty than had been recognized. Kunsberg's experience had been first in combatting pornography and the Mafia, followed by initiatory Washington service in the office of the general counsel of the Central Intelligence Agency, Judge Stanley Sporkin, rather than in arms control or treaty interpretation. Building on Harris's approach, he prepared a nineteen-page report with a radically revised interpretation of the ABM Treaty. His reading, going beyond Harris's, would have allowed not only development and testing but even deployment of systems based on new physical principles. Perle and Iklé seized on this interpretation and promptly sought approval from the interagency arms control committee at a meeting on September 17. The matter was then taken to the legal adviser of the Department of State, Abraham D. Sofaer, who had been named to the post by Shultz not long before from his previous position as a judge of the U.S. District Court in New York City. It was also referred to the office of the general counsel of the Department of Defense and to the general counsel of the Arms Control and Disarmament Agency, Thomas Graham, Jr.

Judge Sofaer, as he prefers to be titled, turned the matter over to three young attorneys he had brought with him into government service a few weeks earlier, cutting out the experienced career State Department lawyer who had long worked in this field, Michael J. Matheson. They found flaws in Kunsberg's analysis, particularly on the question of allowed deployment. But a hasty review of the

Rand, raised ABM Treaty interpretation issues. Although at that time nothing came of either the compliance or interpretation issues, both later resurfaced. By late 1984, Pillsbury was working in Iklé's office. Pillsbury's continuing interest in Soviet compliance issues, and that of Jones and others in U.S. SDI testing, combined and led to Harris's reinvolvement in ABM Treaty interpretation. And Paul Nitze, who had no doubts about the traditional interpretation in 1977, or even in May 1985, had a change of view in September–October 1985.

negotiating record and consultation with Ambassador Paul H. Nitze, the only member of the Strategic Arms Limitation Talks (SALT) I ABM Treaty negotiating team serving in the Reagan administration, led Sofaer to decide the record could be used to support the broader interpretation on development and testing.[7] He so reported to Shultz and Nitze on October 3. The very next day, the high-level interagency Special Arms Control Policy Group, chaired by McFarlane, met and discussed the issue. The Defense Department (Iklé and Perle) quickly abandoned the extreme Kunsberg interpretation and accepted Sofaer's. When the meeting ended, McFarlane called for a new position paper to set forth and discuss the broader interpretation.[8]

It is unclear whether McFarlane sought and obtained the president's approval before his public remarks two days later on national television, or whether—as is more likely—he acted on his own. In either case his action was impulsive and short-circuited serious review of the matter and its implications. The agency representatives, Ambassador Nitze, and at least one principal, Secretary

7. The review by Sofaer and his three associates lasted only two and a half weeks. During this time they were unable to locate all the relevant negotiating history and did not adequately review known records on subsequent practice. Only after the decision had been made did they prepare an incomplete memorandum on the ratification record that Sofaer himself later disavowed. Incidentally, although he was given the Kunsberg paper by the Defense Department, Sofaer was not given or even advised of the existence of the Fitzgerald-Graybeal study.

Sofaer was informed by one of his staff researchers, William J. Sims III, that a memorandum by the assistant general counsel of the Department of Defense, John H. McNeill, rejected the proposed reinterpretation; that Thomas Graham, Jr., the general counsel of ACDA, also rejected the interpretation; and that Sims himself had concluded that only the traditional interpretation was justified. Sofaer did not, however, report any of this in his memorandum to Secretary Shultz and Ambassador Nitze.

Sims pointed out many errors in Sofaer's analysis and his selective use of the record. In January 1986 he left Sofaer's office, transferring to the Office of the General Counsel in the Arms Control and Disarmament Agency. There he continued to study the issue and was confirmed in his conclusion that the reinterpretation was not justified. In August 1986, when Sofaer submitted a new, classified report to Congress seeking to justify the new interpretation, Sims filed a memorandum for the record (never released) and resigned from the government.

8. See Oberdorfer, *Washington Post*, October 22, 1985; and David Ignatius, "Maneuvering to Legalize SDI Tests," *Washington Post*, February 6, 1987.

Shultz, did not believe the matter had been settled at the subcabinet level meeting on October 4. Moreover, McFarlane was unaware that the general counsels of the Department of Defense and ACDA did not accept the Sofaer (or Kunsberg) reinterpretations.[9] Launched by Perle and Iklé, the initiative was now one relying essentially on Sofaer, and prematurely accepted and publicly avowed by McFarlane. By his own later admission, Sofaer himself had not at this point seen much of the pertinent negotiating record, studied the ratification proceedings, reviewed subsequent practice of the parties, or consulted the American negotiators (other than Nitze, who changed his previous view to support a new reading of the negotiating record, although he opposed a public change of position by the administration).

The Political Context of the Reinterpretation

Coincidentally, on the very day that Sofaer presented his memorandum, October 3, 1985, six former Democratic and Republican secretaries of defense publicly endorsed the ABM Treaty on the thirteenth anniversary of its coming into force. Harold Brown, Clark Clifford, Melvin Laird, Robert S. McNamara, Elliot Richardson, and James Schlesinger reaffirmed that the treaty "makes an important contribution to American security" and urged both sides to "avoid actions that erode the ABM Treaty."[10]

While the basic motive for the reinterpretation was the administration's desire to proceed untrammeled with the SDI program,

9. The Office of the General Counsel of the Defense Department had found no basis for reinterpretation when it reviewed the subject earlier in the year, nor at that time had anyone else in the U.S. government. Dissatisfied with this situation, Iklé and Perle then decided to assign Kunsberg from their own office to *find* a way to circumvent the treaty constraints. The fact that the Office of the General Counsel of the Department of Defense did not contribute to or endorse the reinterpretation, and that the assistant general counsel had written a memorandum rejecting it, was not raised by Perle and Iklé in the meetings on October 4 and 11.

10. "Six Former Secretaries of Defense Support ABM Treaty," Press Release, Washington, D.C., October 3, 1985.

there was no urgency in terms of that program. The more immediate impetus for the hasty Kunsberg and Sofaer reviews, and McFarlane's precipitate action, was bureaucratic maneuvering in light of the diplomatic calendar. President Reagan had agreed to meet with General Secretary Mikhail Gorbachev at Geneva in November 1985. Weinberger, Iklé, and Perle were worried that the president would agree to some reaffirmation of the ABM Treaty, perhaps for a ten-year period, and wanted to ensure that any such action would not impinge on the SDI. In addition, they may have hoped that a predictably harsh Soviet reaction to the reinterpretation would reduce prospects for any arms agreement and perhaps undermine the ABM Treaty.

Secretary Weinberger lost a minor skirmish on October 11 when the president accepted the equivocal outcome under which the SDI program would continue for the present on the basis of the so-called restrictive (traditional) interpretation, but he won a major victory in the reaffirmation of the validity of the new interpretation as "fully justified." Nonetheless, Weinberger feared a presidential commitment to abide by the narrow interpretation for some extended period. McFarlane, his unintended confederate, had in fact probably pushed through the reinterpretation, not because he wished to undermine the ABM Treaty, but because he wanted it as a bargaining chip to use in negotiations with the Soviets for a compromise strategic arms reduction agreement. The progenitors of the new interpretation thus had contradictory purposes. Accordingly, after Reagan had decided (on the concurrent advice of Donald Regan, Shultz, and McFarlane) that the defense secretary would not accompany him to Geneva, Weinberger sent a letter to Reagan, leaked publicly the very day the president arrived in Geneva, strongly urging him not to agree to any limitation. His "top-unclassified" letter read, in part: "In Geneva, you will almost certainly come under great pressure . . . to agree formally to limit SDI research, development, and testing to only that research allowed under the most restrictive interpretation of the ABM Treaty, even though you have determined that a less restrictive interpretation is justified legally." He then couched the point in terms calculated to affect Reagan's response: "The Soviets doubtless will seek assurances that you will continue to be bound to such tight limits on SDI development and testing that would discourage the Congress from making any but token appropriations."[11]

No agreement was reached at Geneva except to continue negotiations.

The October 11 compromise prevented an immediate issue from arising on Capitol Hill, since the SDI authorization and appropriations continued to be framed in terms compatible with the traditional interpretation of the ABM Treaty. Nonetheless, disquiet remained. Hearings were held by a House Foreign Affairs Committee subcommittee on October 22 and by the Senate Armed Services Committee on November 21, 1985. At these hearings, the elements of the contending positions were laid out for the first time in public, by Sofaer and Nitze for the administration, and by former negotiators who challenged the reinterpretation, particularly Ambassador Gerard C. Smith, who had headed the SALT ABM Treaty negotiating team, and John B. Rhinelander, who had been legal adviser to the U.S. delegation.[12]

During the months that followed, Senator Sam Nunn (D-Georgia), the influential ranking Democrat on the Senate Armed Services Committee, and other senators pressed the administration for the release to the Senate, on a classified basis, of the negotiating record. The administration witnesses claimed that it supported the case for reinterpretation, while the former negotiators contended that it did not. In August 1986 the administration finally released under strict rules of access a large file of relevant excerpts from that record accompanied by a new, classified report by Sofaer. This action prompted several senators to object again to the new interpretation,

11. "Text of Weinberger's Letter," *Washington Post,* November 17, 1985.

An anonymous senior "White House official" accompanying President Reagan, asked by journalists whether the Weinberger letter was designed to sabotage the summit, replied: "Sure it was." The official was McFarlane.

12. *ABM Treaty Interpretation Dispute,* Hearing before the Subcommittee on Arms Control, International Security and Science of the House Committee on Foreign Affairs, 99 Cong. 1 sess. (GPO, 1986), 382 pp.; and *Strategic Defense Initiative,* Hearings before the Subcommittee on Strategic and Theater Nuclear Forces of the Senate Committee on Armed Services, 99 Cong. 1 sess. (GPO, 1986), 425 pp.

particularly after the Reykjavik summit meeting in October 1986 drew attention to the issue of ABM Treaty obligations as a key factor in the U.S.-Soviet impasse over the SDI blocking agreement on strategic arms reductions.

The Reykjavik summit, with its apparent near agreement on far-reaching strategic arms limitations, stirred up considerable interest in finding some compromise on the SDI. That, in turn, led Secretary Weinberger in early 1987 to propose both adoption of the new treaty interpretation (now labelled "*the* legally correct interpretation," or "LCI" in informal terms within the administration) as the guideline for the SDI program, and early deployment of some ballistic missile defense system. Weinberger, with support from Patrick Buchanan, sought to get a presidential call for early deployment in the State of the Union address in January 1987, but that was foiled by the new national security adviser, Frank Carlucci, on the grounds that no decision had yet been made. A National Security Planning Group (inner National Security Council) meeting of Shultz and Weinberger with President Reagan was held on February 3. While Reagan seemed reluctant to move toward early deployment, he was more willing to consider full adoption of the new interpretation.[13] By this time, Attorney General Edwin Meese III had been asked for his advice, and after a quick review by the Office of the Legal Counsel (Charles J. Cooper, who had also given the desired answer to questions about the Iranian arms-for-hostages deal), Meese blessed the ABM reinterpretation. Shultz, who argued vigorously against early deployment, evidently felt he could not also prevail on the issue of interpretation at that time. Accordingly, in line with a position advised by both Sofaer and Nitze, he urged a delay for more detailed studies of the record. That was the president's decision. He signed National Security Decision Directive (NSDD)–261, which outlined a schedule for new studies and consultations with the allies and Congress, directed toward paving the way for full adoption of the permissive reinterpretation. This

13. Weinberger and Perle were probably more interested in getting approval for the reinterpretation than for early deployment and may have hoped that the president would at least "split the difference" by approving the application of the new interpretation. That was precisely his inclination.

new compromise bought time, but it also moved further toward adoption and application of the broad interpretation.

Minutes of the meeting were leaked, showing that the Joint Chiefs of Staff had not supported Weinberger in seeking a decision on early deployment. Shultz, joining the JCS, commented that "the chiefs have been skeptical on going back on the ABM Treaty." Reagan inquired about the Soviet reaction, and Shultz expressed uncertainty, but Weinberger argued "We shouldn't debate with the Soviets what can and can't be prohibited." Reagan summed up his own view in terms ominous for the future and apparently uncorrected by anyone present who may have been better informed: "Why don't we just go ahead on the assumption that this is what we're doing and it's right." He also said, evidently with reference to an earlier comment by Shultz that the United States should "feel out" the Soviet reaction, "Don't ask the Soviets. Tell them."[14]

Consultations with the Soviet Union

President Reagan's offhand remarks at the meeting of February 3, 1987, were promptly translated into a statement of administration policy by Secretary Shultz. He advised the House Appropriations Committee on February 11 that "we don't think any further negotiations are necessary" with the Soviet Union on the matter of interpretation of the treaty, and that the administration planned to proceed on the basis of "what we think it says."[15] This testimony came the day after a second high-level White House meeting on February 10 that confirmed the general conclusion of the February 3 meeting and set a speeded timetable for completion of the new

14. Gregory A. Fossedal, "NSC Minutes Show President Leaning to SDI Deployment," *Washington Times,* February 6, 1987. The authenticity of the minutes was implicitly confirmed by a subsequent inconclusive FBI investigation of who had leaked them to the conservative newspaper.

15. See R. Jeffrey Smith and Joanne Omang, "Form of ABM Consultations Not Settled, Shultz Says; Talks with Soviets Ruled Out; Administration Will Proceed on 'What We Think It Says,' " *Washington Post,* February 12, 1987.

studies and "consultations" on the new interpretation with the Congress and the European allies.

Shultz's reference to any "*further* negotiations" with the Soviets implied there had been some. In fact, from the very outset in September–October 1985 there were none. Under accepted international practice, a question of material interpretation of obligations under a treaty, especially if it involves a change in existing practice or would have the effect of an amendment, should be discussed and agreed upon by the parties. In addition, Article XIII of the ABM Treaty had set up a body and procedures expressly for considering "questions concerning compliance with the obligations assumed and related situations which may be considered ambiguous": the Standing Consultative Commission (SCC).[16] In any case, whether through the SCC or other diplomatic contact, the question should have been raised with the Soviet Union before any of the chain of U.S. government pronouncements, beginning with McFarlane's "Meet the Press" comment. Only after the White House confirmation of a new interpretation on October 8 and 14 was the Soviet Embassy routinely informed of the new American position. There was no inquiry into the Soviet interpretation, nor offer to discuss the matter.[17]

Soviet spokesmen, in particular Marshal Sergei Sokolov, then the defense minister, and Marshal Sergei Akhromeyev, his first deputy and chief of the General Staff, both promptly and vigorously reaffirmed the traditional interpretation, discussing the relevant provisions in detail, and flatly rejected the validity of the broad interpretation.[18]

16. See the discussion in section VI below.

17. Information from American and Soviet diplomatic sources.

In November 1985, when asked in a Senate hearing about bringing the matter to the SCC, Sofaer blandly commented, "No one in the administration so far as I know has made such a decision or addressed himself to that question"—as though it were not in part his job. (See *Strategic Defense Initiative*, Hearings, p. 175.)

In May 1987 the Soviet Embassy was informed of the new position by the State Department just before the public release of the Sofaer report of May 11, 1987 (see note 22 below). But it had not been consulted about release of portions of the classified negotiating record.

18. See section IV below under "Soviet Statements." Interestingly, Marshal

The Reagan administration's failure to consult the Soviet Union on the interpretation issue is more than just a question of diplomatic etiquette, or even propriety. One of the main arguments advanced for the new interpretation is that the Soviets might not consider themselves bound by the traditional interpretation, thus placing the United States at a disadvantage if it bound itself to a "double standard" restrictive reading while the Soviets did not.[19] Of course, the best way to have determined whether the Soviets considered themselves bound to the traditional restrictive interpretation would obviously have been to ask them for a clear recommitment. If they did not agree that the traditional interpretation was the correct one, the United States could then have adopted a broader reading, or sought to negotiate agreement on the traditional or any new basis to ensure that both would be bound by the same obligations. The administration did not take this path because it knew that the Soviet government would in fact strongly reaffirm the traditional interpretation, making it much more difficult for the United States to free its hands for SDI testing.

Congressional and Allied Reaction

Of far greater concern to the Reagan administration than the strong Soviet rejection was the almost equally negative reaction of key congressional leaders and of America's principal European allies.

The first important congressional response was a twelve-page letter from Senator Carl Levin (D-Michigan) on December 1, 1986,

---

Akhromeyev had attacked and emphatically rejected the heart of the broad reinterpretation—that is, to construe Agreed Statement D as modifying Article V and allowing development and testing of space-based systems based on new physical principles—in *Pravda* on June 4, 1985, four months *before* McFarlane's statement. Yet neither Shultz nor anyone else mentioned this authoritative previous Soviet rejection of the broad interpretation, nor the many that had followed after the American announcements in October 1985, when on February 3, 1987, President Reagan asked about the Soviet reaction.

19. See, for example, Paul Nitze, *ABM Treaty Interpretation Dispute*, Hearing, p. 352; and *Congressional Record*, daily edition (May 19, 1987), p. S6624.

later publicly released by the senator. Then on February 6, 1987, as soon as the press reported the renewed high-level consideration of the broad reading, Senator Nunn publicly warned President Reagan that the administration would provoke a "constitutional confrontation of profound dimensions" if it adopted the reinterpretation without consulting Congress and obtaining a consensus on the change.[20]

By the time of the second White House meeting on February 10, a week after the first, statements of concern had been made by a number of allies, including again messages from Prime Minister Margaret Thatcher of Great Britain and Chancellor Helmut Kohl of West Germany, Lord Peter Carrington, Secretary General of NATO, and from Japan, Canada, and others. Even before the meeting, the president had authorized Shultz to say publicly that consultations would be held with the allies and the Senate before a decision was made to implement the broader interpretation of the ABM Treaty, and those commitments were confirmed at the meeting. Yet the nature of the consultations remained undecided even afterward. Some members of the administration openly commented that while the allies had made clear that "they don't like the broad interpretation," their views would not count for a great deal because they did not have access to the negotiating record and were not qualified to interpret the treaty.[21] Ambassador Nitze and Assistant Secretary of Defense Perle were dispatched to London, Bonn, Paris, Rome, Brussels, and The Hague in late February to register the administration's interest in pursuing the broad interpretation. They were coolly received.

The congressional reaction was less easy for the White House to contain. New Senate hearings in March strongly challenged the administration's position, and most damaging was a strong, in-

20. See Michael R. Gordon, "Reagan Is Warned by Senator Nunn over ABM Treaty," New York Times, February 7, 1987; and Gordon, "U.S. Said to Near Decision on Sense of '72 ABM Treaty," New York Times, February 5, 1987. The press account erroneously cited Nunn as having referred to a constitutional "crisis" rather than "confrontation."

21. ACDA Director Kenneth L. Adelman, cited in Smith and Omang, Washington Post, February 12, 1987.

formed refutation by Senator Nunn, based among other things on his detailed review of the classified negotiating record provided by the administration. Also, the bipartisan group of six former secretaries of defense who had endorsed the ABM Treaty in October of 1985 urged the administration on March 9, 1987, to "continue to adhere to the traditional interpretation" as observed by both sides since 1972. A similar statement supporting the traditional interpretation was signed by eight principal negotiators of the treaty (but not, of course, by Nitze).

On May 13, 1987, the Department of State released a declassified and substantially revised version of Sofaer's August 1986 classified study of the negotiating record, including declassified versions of or excerpts from a large number of documents.[22] Six days later Senator Nunn released (with administration declassification) his own analysis, a devastating rebuttal, updated quickly to take account of Sofaer's newly released version.[23]

The issues, and a major part of the record, were now on the table for public consideration.

Summing Up the Issue

At this writing the matter of the reinterpretation of the ABM Treaty advanced by the Reagan administration has not been resolved. Clearly it is both a legal matter of rules and evidence on treaty interpretation and a political issue. It should not, however, be a question of political loyalty to the policy preference, convenience, or determination of an administration. For there are matters

22. Office of the Legal Adviser, Department of State, "The ABM Treaty—Part I: Treaty Language and Negotiating History," May 11, 1987, 82 pp. plus a 100-page appendix of declassified documents, reprinted in its entirety in the *Congressional Record*, daily edition (May 19, 1987), pp. S6623–63. (Hereafter cited in text and notes as Sofaer, *Cong. Rec.*, May 19, 1987.)

23. Senator Sam Nunn, "Interpretation of the ABM Treaty—Part Four: An Examination of Judge Sofaer's Analysis of the Negotiating Record," May 19, 1987, 157 pp., reprinted in its entirety in the *Congressional Record*, daily edition (May 20, 1987), pp. S6809–31. (Hereafter cited in texts and notes as Nunn, *Cong. Rec.*, May 20, 1987.)

of historical fact, of evidence as to the meaning of the treaty, that must be examined and weighed.

According to the canons of legal interpretation, the first and strongest evidence is the express language of a treaty. This means the *letter* of a treaty, not its spirit. The *purpose* of the treaty is, however, relevant in determining the meaning of the language. Language must be interpreted in good faith. Only if the language is not sufficiently clear does one go on to the next step, review of *subsequent practice*. Subsequent practice includes subsequent statements and subsequent actions of the parties. Normally, only if subsequent practice is unclear does one include review of the *negotiating record,* to determine the intent and the understanding of the parties, particularly as conveyed by their negotiators as they agreed upon the language of the treaty, and evidence on the meaning held by those involved in the *ratification process,* including the representatives of the executive and the legislative branches.

The Sofaer reinterpretation violated this established process. The express language of the treaty was challenged on the basis of the logic of its construction rather than its intent. Then a reconstruction of the logic of the language was justified by a reading of parts of the negotiating record. Subsequent practice had not been given more than superficial review before the new interpretation was adopted. Contrary judgments of most of the professional counsel in *all* departments—Defense, State, and ACDA—were overridden and not even brought to the attention of policymakers before a position was prematurely announced, and then legitimated by a hasty decision. Subsequent efforts have concentrated on justifying a decision already made, and convenient to the administration's other purposes (minimizing constraints on the SDI program), rather than on weighing the evidence.

The White House decisionmaking process was casual and inadequate. There was no internal testing of the validity of the new interpretation. Negative evidence was suppressed. Neither Cabinet-level review, nor review with the president, was undertaken before the new policy was adopted and made public. There was no consultation with Congress. There was no consultation with or information to the allies. There was no consultation with or even advance notification of the other party to the treaty, the Soviet Union. But, then, there was no adequate consultation even within the administration itself—even with the president.

The treaty language, the negotiating record, the ratification process, and subsequent practice must now be examined to judge the merits of the case for reinterpretation.

II

The ABM Treaty Constraints
on Future Systems

IN EXAMINING the text of a treaty, the most important facts are the effect of the language, intent of the parties, and purpose of the provisions. The interrelation and mutually reinforcing effect of the several provisions in its articles (and related agreed statements expanding on them) are also important. Judge Sofaer in effect turns the process of interpretation of the text on its head: instead of interpreting the terms of the treaty as a whole, he disaggregates and then reassembles them, often with great violence to the clear meaning of the language. Bending the parts to fit his preferred pattern, he constructs a kind of ABM Treaty Mod II, "Made in the USA," to suit the needs of a policy giving priority to the Reagan administration's SDI program, rather than to the intent and purpose of the United States and the Soviet Union when together they concluded the ABM Treaty.

Five provisions of the treaty are of central significance to understanding the constraints on "future" ABM systems and components based on "other physical principles."

Article I(2), while virtually ignored in the reinterpretation, is directly relevant. That article provides: "Each Party undertakes not to deploy ABM systems for a defense of the territory of its country and not to provide a base for such a defense, and not to deploy ABM systems for defense of an individual region except as provided for in Article III of this Treaty."

Article I(2) lays down a flat ban on deploying any ABM system capable of providing a nationwide defense of the United States or the Soviet Union, regardless of the types of technologies used, and apart from two small ABM system deployment sites (now one) allowed to each party for regional defense under Article III. Moreover, it bans creation of a "base" for such a defense. The implications of this broad Article I(2) constraint will be discussed later.[1]

Article II lays out definitions. Paragraph 1 states: "For the purpose of this Treaty an ABM system is a system to counter strategic ballistic missiles or their elements in flight trajectory, currently consisting of: (a) ABM interceptor missiles . . . ; (b) ABM launchers . . . ; and (c) ABM radars. . . ." Note that an ABM system is defined by its purpose, not by its components. It is *any* system for that purpose.

By stating that ABM systems "currently" (in 1972) consisted of interceptor missiles, launchers, and radars, the text clearly recognizes that ABM systems *could* be constituted of other components; otherwise, the qualification "currently" would not have been stipulated. Also note that the comma before "currently" makes the listed components illustrative, not restrictive.

Article III contains an explicit exception to the treaty's prohibitions, allowing limited regional deployments of a fixed land-based ABM system. It describes the type and number of ABM launchers, interceptor missiles, and radars that each party may deploy at two small (150-km radius) sites—one around its capital and one at a

---

1. Article I(2) stemmed from a Soviet initiative. Soviet interpretations of the treaty place great weight on the effect of this article in precluding any system capable of defending "the territory" of a party—for example, any system for interception of ballistic missiles in the boost phase of their trajectory, in contradistinction to systems for terminal defense of an "individual region" mentioned in the second clause and dealt with in Article III.

missile launch site.[2] Its details are not relevant to the reinterpretation issue, but the lead-in clause of the article is: "Each Party undertakes not to deploy ABM systems or their components except . . ." as then specified in detail. All other deployment is banned.

Because Article III exempts from its deployment ban only the *existing* ABM launchers, interceptor missiles, and radars specified in its subsections, it is clear that the article prohibits deployment of *future* ABM systems and components based on other physical principles.

Article V(1) provides: "Each Party undertakes not to develop, test, or deploy ABM systems or components which are sea-based, air-based, space-based, or mobile land-based."

The United States intended Article V(1) to cover all mobile basing modes, current and future, and the delegation and Washington decisionmakers believed in 1972 (and until October 1985) that the text does so.

Agreed Statement D, while not a part of the text, is a formally agreed interpretive understanding having the same binding legal effect as the body of the treaty itself.[3] The full text reads:

> In order to insure fulfillment of the obligation not to deploy ABM systems and their components except as provided in Article III of the Treaty, the Parties agree that in the event ABM systems based on other physical principles and including components capable of substituting for ABM interceptor missiles, ABM launchers, or ABM radars are created in the future, specific limitations on such systems and their components would be subject to discussion in accordance with Article XIII and agreement in accordance with Article XIV of the Treaty.

As the introductory clause states, the purpose of Agreed State-

---

2. The ABM Treaty in 1972 permitted each party two deployment areas with 100 ABM launchers and deployed interceptors and ABM radars in each. By a protocol amending the treaty, signed in 1974 and ratified in 1976, this allowance was reduced to one deployment area for each side.

3. This Agreed Statement was formally initialed by the heads of the two delegations on May 26, 1972, and accepted by both sides as binding.

The letter designation "D" was a later American editorial convenience, and indeed from 1972 to 1980 it was listed as "E" in official records. Soviet commentators since October 1985 have in practice accepted the "D" designation.

ment D is to reinforce the strict deployment limitations imposed by Article III. Although it does not spell out the other restrictions imposed by the treaty, it is predicated on them. Thus the parties, in envisaging the possible creation in the future of ABM systems incorporating ABM components based on new technologies ("other physical principles" than those embodied in ABM interceptor missiles, launchers, and radars), recognized that it would be necessary to consult and agree upon amendment to the treaty in order to determine allowed limited deployment in keeping with the treaty's restrictive purpose. In order not to impinge unduly on technological development, the "threshold" was set at new components capable of substituting for and performing the function of the three existing components. Other devices short of that threshold and capable of performing adjunct or subcomponent functions could be developed, tested, and used in deployed systems.

In view of the constraints of Article III (and in keeping with the objective set forth in Article I), no deployment would be allowed except under agreed amendment.

In view of the more far-reaching constraints of Article V, any new ABM components that could be created (developed and tested) would be limited to components of fixed, land-based ABM systems. While that is not explicit, it is clear. Agreed Statement D was designed to reinforce Article III, not to modify or diminish Article V or any other article.

Apparently it was the fact that only Agreed Statement D specifically *referred* to "future" ABM systems and components, and to "other physical principles," that first drew the attention of Harris, Kunsberg, and then Sofaer to the possibility of reinterpreting the treaty by claiming that no part of the treaty itself, but only D, *applied* to future systems and components. This reconstruction required ignoring Article I and reinterpreting Articles II(1), III, and V(1). (Kunsberg's broadest reading would also have reinterpreted Agreed Statement D itself to claim that there was no binding constraint even on deployment of future ABM systems or components, but Sofaer stopped short of that,[4] and the administration's reinterpretation accepts the ban on deployment.)

4. In his submission of May 11, 1987, Sofaer notes the "even broader view,"

By relegating future systems exclusively to Agreed Statement D and reconstruing the definitions in Article II(1), the reinterpretation reads both Article III and Article V(1) as applying to conventional technologies only. Thus Sofaer argues that Article III really bans only "the deployment of all fixed land-based systems and components derived from current technological principles, except as specifically permitted."[5] How he reaches this circumscribed meaning requires review of the remaining provisions, but it is simply—and almost self-evidently—contrived.

Sofaer interprets the overlap between the ban on deploying systems based on other physical principles except after consultation and amendment, in Agreed Statement D, and the ban on deployment except as permitted in Article III, as "rendering a portion of the treaty superfluous." He claims that it therefore "violates accepted canons of construction" in treaty interpretation. But there is no rule in international treaty law against consistent redundancy. His reinterpretation, he argues, establishes a "coherent non-redundant scheme." In doing this, however, Sofaer ignores the stated relationship between the two prohibitions: Agreed Statement D opens with the words "In order to insure fulfillment of the obligation not to deploy ABM systems and their components except as provided in Article III of the Treaty," making clear that the intent was to reinforce the obligation already

---

or third interpretation, advanced earlier by Kunsberg. Although he does not adopt it, he argues that this even broader interpretation "is not precluded by the text," because Agreed Statement D does not "explicitly prohibit the Parties from deploying OPP [other physical principle] devices until they agree on specific limitations." Sofaer concedes, however, in understatement, that "the language of the Treaty casts grave doubt on this interpretation," and that it would "leave a substantial gap in the Treaty's coverage and thereby potentially undermine its most fundamental Purpose." (Sofaer, *Cong. Rec.,* May 19, 1987, p. S6625.) Presumably Sofaer resurrects Kunsberg's thesis in order to make his own reinterpretation appear more moderate and reasonable, "centered" between the traditional restrictive and the "even broader" views. He fails to acknowledge that the very argument about opening a substantial gap in coverage and potentially undermining the purpose of the treaty applies to his own interpretation as well.

5. *ABM Treaty Interpretation Dispute,* Hearing before the Subcommittee on Arms Control, International Security and Science of the House Committee on Foreign Affairs, 99 Cong. 1 sess. (Government Printing Office, 1986), pp. 14–15.

established in Article III. Sofaer also fails to acknowledge other formal redundancies (including those between Articles I and III), including redundancies in his own constructive interpretation, some of which will be noted briefly later.

In his initial testimony, Sofaer felt obliged to concede that "Article V(1) is clear on its face: it says no development, testing, or deployment of 'ABM systems or components' other than those that are fixed land-based." But he argues that "this language does not settle the issue of the article's applicability to future systems or components" because "that issue depends on the meaning of the term 'ABM systems and components,' "[6] in other words on Article II(1). That is a valid point.

As for Article II(1), however, Sofaer argues that while "proponents of the restrictive view contend that this definition is functional," and is "plausible, . . . it is not the only reasonable reading." Indeed, "the provision can more reasonably be read to mean that the systems contemplated by the Treaty are those that serve the functions described and that currently consist of the listed components."[7] This is a typical example of Sofaer's interpretative method. First he asserts (but does not demonstrate) that alternative interpretations are possible and reasonable, then he argues (without substantiation) that the restrictive interpretation is less reasonable than the alternatives because it does not fit his overall pattern of interpretation. But to support his position he ignores the plain meaning of the comma and phrase ", *currently* consisting of" and then replaces it with his own quite different language—omitting the comma and inserting "and."[8] The language in Article II(1) is quite clear on its face: the three components

6. *ABM Treaty Interpretation Dispute*, Hearing, p. 12.

7. Ibid., pp. 12–13.

8. Pressed by Senator Nunn on the liberty he was taking by substituting "and" for the comma before "currently," changing an appositive clause into an independent and additive one, Sofaer went so far as to argue "it makes more sense to put the word 'and' in." Senator Nunn, incredulous, asked: "Are you saying it makes more sense to use the word 'and'?" Judge Sofaer: "Yes; to read it as though the word 'and' was there, certainly." (*Strategic Defense Initiative*, Hearings before the Subcommittee on Strategic and Theater Nuclear Forces of the Senate Armed Services Committee, 99. Cong. 1 sess. [GPO, 1986], p. 179.)

identified and named are only those "currently" constituting ABM systems; they do not constitute a comprehensive and exclusionary listing.

Thus Sofaer's reinterpretation requires reshaping several provisions of the treaty in order to make them fit into his own novel construct. Moreover, all elements of Sofaer's reconstruction must stand up to make the case that the treaty excludes any coverage of future technologies except as provided in Agreed Statement D. For this reason, my review of the negotiating record will cover the full range of articles critical to the reinterpretation.

The reinterpretation also flies in the face of the whole purpose of the ABM Treaty—a treaty designed for unlimited duration, and with the express objective of precluding a nationwide defense of the two countries by restricting permitted deployments to a specified minimum. Yet the reinterpretation would allow development and testing of future space-based, air-based, sea-based, and mobile land-based ABM systems and components based on other physical principles. This covers the systems of greatest interest to the SDI and most suitable for a nationwide defense.

This discussion essentially summarizes the divergence between the 1985 broad interpretation, and the traditional or restrictive interpretation. It seems highly likely, based on available indications, that most legal scholars, after an examination in good faith of the language of the treaty, seen in terms of its purpose, would reject the case for revising the interpretation.[9] No further review of the record would even seem necessary. Sofaer, however, concluded that the text of the treaty showed "ambiguities" sufficient to justify seeking "guidance" from "the negotiating record

9. Several legal specialists have examined the reinterpretation and found it seriously wanting. See, in particular, Abram Chayes and Antonia Handler Chayes, "Testing and Development of 'Exotic' Systems under the ABM Treaty: The Great Reinterpretation Caper," *Harvard Law Review,* vol. 99 (June 1986), pp. 1956–71; Alan B. Sherr, *A Legal Analysis of the 'New Interpretation' of the Anti-Ballistic Missile Treaty* (Boston: Lawyer's Alliance for Nuclear Arms Control, 1986), 28 pp.; and Kevin C. Kennedy, "Treaty Interpretation by the Executive Branch: The ABM Treaty and 'Star Wars' Testing and Development," *American Journal of International Law,* vol. 80 (October 1986), pp. 854–77.

to see which of the possible constructions most accurately reflects the parties' intentions."[10]

Under standard procedures of treaty interpretation, the next recourse, if it is necessary to go beyond the text of the treaty itself, is not the negotiating record, but subsequent practice. Nonetheless, for reasons of exposition as well as Sofaer's approach, I shall turn first to the negotiating record and then to subsequent practice.

10. *ABM Treaty Interpretation Dispute*, Hearing, p. 15.

III

The Negotiating Record

THE Strategic Arms Limitation Talks (SALT), dealing with limitations on both antiballistic missile systems and strategic offensive arms, began on November 17, 1969.[1] In this discussion I am concerned only with the ABM negotiations. From their beginning until August 17, 1971, those negotiations dealt generally with "ABM systems and components," or with specific constraints in terms of then-current ABM system components based on familiar physical principles.

The Issue of Future Systems

During July and the first half of August of 1971 a debate took place among the agencies in Washington (and within the U.S. SALT negotiating delegation) over proposing a ban on future ABM

1. A brief explanation of the way in which the negotiations were conducted will be helpful in understanding the relevant negotiating history. The U.S. delegation was headed by Ambassador Gerard C. Smith, the director of the Arms Control and Disarmament Agency, and included senior members or delegates

systems.[2] On August 12, President Nixon decided to call for a ban on development, production, testing, and deployment of sea-based, air-based, space-based, and mobile land-based ABM components. These included not only ABM launchers, ABM interceptor missiles, and ABM radars, but also any components able to perform the functions of those three familiar components.[3] In contrast, only

from the Defense Department (Paul Nitze), the State Department (Ambassador J. Graham Parsons), the Joint Chiefs of Staff (Lieutenant General Royal Allison), and a prominent former (and subsequent) Defense official and scientist (Dr. Harold Brown). I was the executive officer, as well as deputy director of the Office of Politico-Military Affairs in the Department of State. The alternate executive officer, Sidney Graybeal, was from ACDA. The full staff, including clerical support and marine guards, numbered about one hundred.

Formal plenary meetings of the two delegations (or, rather, of about a dozen senior representatives from each delegation) were initially held twice a week, then less often as the work intensified. They were used for formal, set piece presentations of proposals, positions, and supporting arguments. Informal conversations between counterparts on the two sides usually followed these sessions.

A series of less formal groups were used for negotiation and working out of agreed texts. Thus an Ad Hoc Working Group existed in August–September 1971, headed by Sidney Graybeal and Viktor Karpov, and it worked on Article II and successfully negotiated Article V. From early in the negotiations, some matters were negotiated by the executive officers (or general secretaries), Nikolai Kishilov and myself. This was later supplemented by meetings of "the Four," Ambassador Parsons and Oleg Grinevsky, joining Kishilov and myself, and "the Three," Kishilov, Grinevsky, and myself. In these groups, Articles I, II, III, and Agreed Statement D, among others, were negotiated. Relevant specifics are noted in the text following.

In all of these exchanges, the actual negotiators were of course representatives of the delegations, receiving instructions and reporting to the senior delegation. The senior delegation, meeting daily and often multiple times daily, was composed of Ambassador Smith, Nitze, Parsons, Allison, Brown, and myself.

2. This debate is partially covered by Sofaer in his May 11 report, but not in a balanced or adequate fashion. For example, he notes that Ambassador J. Graham Parsons "objected" to the proposed ban on future systems. While it is true that Ambassador Parsons recommended to the undersecretary of state against the proposal, I sent a contrary recommendation (each of us aware of the divergent recommendations), and most important Undersecretary John Irwin III, representing the Department of State in the Washington deliberations, also strongly supported the proposal. Sofaer does not note these facts. He also neglects to mention SALT delegate Harold Brown's strong recommendation for a complete ban on future systems. The divergencies in American views before the president reached a firm decision is not, however, relevant to the reinterpretation issue, and need not be pursued further here.

3. National Security Decision Memorandum (NSDM) 127, August 12, 1971.

the *deployment* of future components of fixed land-based systems (such as lasers) would be banned. On August 17, after preparing appropriate draft treaty language and clearing it with Washington, the U.S. delegation submitted a draft article to the Soviets. Because it is crucial to the interpretation issue, its text is cited in full:

Article 6 (1) Each Party undertakes not to deploy ABM systems using devices other than ABM interceptor missiles, ABM launchers, or ABM radars to perform the functions of these components.

(2) Each Party undertakes not to develop or produce for or test or deploy in sea-based, air-based, space-based or mobile land-based modes,

—ABM interceptor missiles,

—ABM launchers,

—ABM radars, or

—other devices to perform the functions of these components.[4]

This article was later renumbered Article V, and the final version reflects a negotiated redraft of the original 6(2) as V(1); as discussed

---

4. From U.S. Delegation A-408, August 17, 1971.

The written record of the negotiations is contained principally in Memoranda of Conversation (memcons, for short), used to report not only on conversations between members of the two delegations, but also on meetings of representatives for negotiation. All formal records of meetings, papers presented or received, and memcons were transmitted to the interested agencies in Washington by "airgrams" (in fact, in typed form, in the diplomatic pouch) with "A-000" identifying numbers. In all some 1,000 A-memoranda were filed in the SALT I negotiation from November 1969 through May 1972, in which the ABM Treaty and Interim Agreement were negotiated. Shorter versions of particularly important materials were sent by encrypted telegram over the Department of State communications network (with U.S. Del SALT 000 designations), and instructions from Washington were similarly sent by cable (State 000000 designations).

It should be borne in mind that except for papers exchanged, there is no common or verbatim record of the negotiations. Each side took such notes and prepared such memoranda as it found useful. Memoranda were usually dictated or written as soon after a discussion as was practical, but they are not transcripts of exchanges.

Draft Article 6(3) is omitted because it does not figure in the reinterpretation. It banned multiple-missile launchers and automatic or rapid reload. It was agreed upon and became Article V(2) of the final text.

below, Article 6(1) was for several months proposed as V(3) and in revised form ultimately became Agreed Statement D.

Sofaer notes that the word "devices" was used in both August subparagraphs to refer to future systems capable of performing the functions of the then-current components listed. He then argues that the *absence* of the word "devices" in the final language of Article V(1)—the descendant of draft Article 6(2)—means that the U.S. negotiators in the end failed to obtain it in the treaty text. This argument is faulty on several counts. For one thing, the United States did not distinguish "devices" (as a code word meaning future) from "components" (meaning traditional ABM launchers, ABM interceptor missiles, and ABM radars). Indeed, while the word "devices" was used in both subparagraphs 6(1) and 6(2) presented on August 17, 1971, the NSDM 127 instruction to the delegation on which they were based did not use the word "devices" anywhere in the paragraph describing mobile systems; it referred to "ABM *components* other than ABM interceptor missiles, ABM launchers, or ABM radars to perform the functions of these components." Nor did the final language of Agreed Statement D, which Sofaer accepts as referring to future systems based on other physical principles, use the word "devices."[5]

The word "devices" was dropped because during the negotiation the U.S. delegation decided that it was too broad a term, one that could constrain and interfere with testing and development of multipurpose technologies. We therefore decided that the treaty text should refer only to ABM systems and components, including references to future *systems* or *components* based on other physical principles and capable of performing the functions of the then-current (1972) types of components of antiballistic missile systems: that is, ABM launchers, interceptor missiles, and radars. Hence it is either a willful or ignorant misstatement on Sofaer's part to say

5. Sofaer deals with this anomaly to his construct by misstatement. In a 1986 article in the *Harvard Law Review*, in discussing this issue he states, "The Soviets later agreed in Agreed Statement D to prohibit the deployment of such *devices* after they were created." (Abraham D. Sofaer, "The ABM Treaty and the Strategic Defense Initiative," *Harvard Law Review*, vol. 99 [June 1986], p. 1980; emphasis added.) But that is untrue. The word "devices" is not used in D, which bans deployment of systems and components, the same words used in Article V(1).

that the absence of "devices" in Article V (originally Article 6) was "language the U.S. negotiators in the end failed to obtain in the Treaty text." (Sofaer, *Cong. Rec.*, May 19, 1987, p. S6627.)

From the outset the U.S. proposals covered two different categories of constraints on future ABM systems based on other physical principles. For mobile systems the U.S. delegation sought a ban on three activities: development, testing, and deployment. For fixed land-based systems, however, we sought a ban on only one activity, deployment. This was in accordance with the delegation's instructions. Also in accordance with those instructions, the delegation did not make the distinction explicit; there was no explicit reference to fixed land-based systems in the U.S. draft proposals for any article (or later agreed statement, either). Thus from August 17 on there was a redundancy in subparagraphs Article 6(1) and 6(2) in that 6(1) banned deployment of devices capable of performing the functions of ABM components, while 6(2) similarly banned such deployment, and development and testing as well, for a designated subclass of systems (mobile).[6]

The Soviet reaction for some time was guarded, with doubts expressed on the need for and feasibility of dealing with unknown systems. There were several reasons for Soviet arguments that such provisions were not "necessary," were "superfluous," or were "premature." But contrary to the Sofaer image the Soviets were not adamant, and indeed as the full negotiating history makes clear, the Soviet position changed significantly over time as they came to *accept* the American position.

Owing to the long dispute in Washington in July and August over what position to adopt on the issue of future systems, the U.S. delegation had submitted a draft ABM Treaty text on July 27, complete except for a mysterious blank Article 6, with the statement that an "appropriate provision" concerning sea-based, space-based, air-based, and mobile land-based ABM systems would be provided later. This lacuna seemed doubly suspicious to the Soviets because earlier both the United States and the Soviet Union had

6. In this instance, Sofaer finds no problem with a glaring redundancy, and the delegation and government in Washington saw no "violation of accepted canons" in it.

presented drafts with similar provisions on mobile systems. Given that it had taken the U.S. government six weeks of intensive debate on the issue, it is hardly surprising that the Soviet side needed some time to consider the matter.

From the beginning the Soviet reaction to the two draft American subparagraphs dealing with future systems differed significantly, a fact obscured by the whole line of argument of Sofaer and other proponents of the reinterpretation. Some of the initial Soviet comments referred generally to the U.S. draft Article 6. But the Soviet negotiators concentrated their attention on Article 6(1), the subparagraph limiting only *deployment* of future systems based on other physical principles. This focus was not immediately noted by the American delegation, because most of the arguments were couched in general terms seeking to elicit the reasons for and intent of the new U.S. proposal. In fact, however, not a single Soviet objection was directed specifically at Article 6(2), with its proposed ban on development, production, testing, and deployment of mobile systems and components.[7] In contrast, apart from general statements that could apply to both paragraphs, there were many objections and questions focused explicitly on Article 6(1), which would ban only deployment, but of fixed land-based systems.

7. In the first four weeks there were indeed few references at all to Article 6(2) on mobile systems. The only substantive one was by Academician Aleksandr Shchukin on August 24, when he inquired about the introduction into Article 6(2) (and also 6(3), not dealing with future systems) of the category of "development," as well as "testing" and "deployment." He inquired as to the "practical implications" of including a ban on development, and "the manner of verifying" such a ban on development. But he did not raise an objection, much less reject it. (A-424, Aug. 24, 1971.)

It was natural that the Soviets should raise these questions. In the previous U.S. draft on mobile ABM systems and components (August 4, 1970) and the previous Soviet drafts of virtually the same provision (December 4, 1970, and March 19, 1971), testing, but *not* development, had been banned along with deployment of sea-based, air-based, space-based, and mobile land-based ABM systems or components. The Soviets accepted "development" on September 17, at the same time agreement was reached on language covering future systems and components.

The United States also introduced the idea of a ban on *production* in its August 17 proposal, but by mid-September when the article was agreed upon we had dropped that idea because of second thoughts on its desirability and verifiability.

Even on the basis of the incomplete portions of the negotiating record released by Sofaer, there are *six* discussions in which Soviet negotiators challenged Article 6(1) and *none* in which Article 6(2) was similarly challenged, in the three weeks after the article was proposed.[8] Apart from Sofaer's argument that the "logic" of opposing consideration of unknown future systems should have applied to both 6(1) and 6(2), and therefore (in his view) *should* have led the Soviets to oppose both equally, and despite his repeated assertions that such was the case, the record—even his selected excerpts from the record—does not support his claim.[9]

Sofaer then argues that "the Soviet proposal itself, Article V(1) of the Soviet draft, implicitly rejected the U.S. position in Article 6(2) of the U.S. draft, because it showed the Soviet intent to regulate ABM missiles, launchers, and radars." (Sofaer, ibid., p. S6628.) But this Soviet language had been drafted months before and was virtually the same as the U.S. language on the subject prior to the July–August revision of the U.S. position. A previous long-standing Soviet proposal can hardly be said to constitute a "rejection" of a new American proposal, even "implicitly." Moreover, the Soviets soon reacted directly—and positively—to the American proposal in Article 6(2).

The Ban on Developing, Testing, and Deploying Future Mobile ABM Systems and Components

On September 8, three weeks after the new U.S. proposal for including ABM systems and components based on future technol-

8. Academician Aleksandr Shchukin, A-424, Aug. 24, 1971; Deputy Foreign Minister Vladimir Semenov, A-438, Aug. 27, 1971; Lieutenant General Konstantin Trusov, A-442, Aug. 31, 1971; General Trusov, A-458, Sept. 3, 1971; Colonel Aleksandr Fedenko, A-481, Sept. 8, 1971; and Mr. Viktor Karpov, A-540, Sept. 8, 1971.

9. Sofaer cites several statements by an *American* negotiator, Sidney Graybeal, from the record in which Graybeal assumed the Soviets objected to both, and a unilateral U.S. working paper he submitted in which the American language on Article 6(2) was bracketed (a device used to register nonagreement) because the Soviet side had not yet accepted the American language. This did not, however, register a *Soviet* expressed difference. Sofaer repeatedly cites this as an "acknowl-

ogy, the Soviet delegation advanced a new formulation for an article on mobile systems that accepted and incorporated the new American proposal, although with fresh and more economical language.

The new Soviet formulation was an undertaking not to test or deploy "mobile land-based, sea-based, air-based or space-based ABM systems and their components," without specifying any types of components, such as ABM interceptor missiles, launchers, or radars. As Soviet negotiator Viktor Karpov noted on September 13, the new Soviet draft "took into account the wishes of the US side." (A-540, Sept. 14, 1971; cited in Nunn, *Cong. Rec.,* May 20, 1987, p. S6814.) Sofaer chose not to mention this statement by Karpov in either his classified statement of August 12, 1986, or his public report of May 11, 1987, and deleted it from the declassified excerpt of the corresponding memcon. As Karpov further explained to his American counterpart, Sidney Graybeal, on September 15, the new formulation "obviates the requirement for the phrase 'other devices for performing the functions of these components' " in the U.S. draft by eliminating any reference to the three then-current components for which future devices could substitute. By simple use of the word "components," unrestricted, any and all ABM components would be covered. (A-503, Sept. 15, 1971.) The approach was attractive, gaining Soviet acceptance of the substance of the American position and cleaning up the tortured American language.

Graybeal specifically checked to ascertain that the Soviet side understood that this new formulation would indeed cover future components based on other physical principles, as had the American proposal. The record of the meeting reports Karpov's unequivocal assurance. "Karpov agreed with Graybeal's interpretation that the Soviet text meant 'any type of present or future components' of ABM systems." (A-503, Sept. 15, 1971.)

The American delegation considered the proposal and unanimously decided that it fully met the U.S. objective and in fact was

---

edgement" of a Soviet position, rather than as an American working assumption as to the Soviet position—one that was proven wrong just a week later, as Graybeal recognized. (Sofaer, *Cong. Rec.,* May 19, 1987, pp. S6628–29.)

preferable to our own stilted language. This judgment was based primarily on the manifest effect of the language, buttressed by Karpov's reassurance that the Soviet side had the same understanding. The paragraph was agreed ad referendum and included without brackets as an agreed provision, now termed Article V(1), in the next version of a consolidated "Joint Draft Text" (JDT) compiled by the two delegations on September 23, 1971. Article V(1) then read, in full and with no bracketed reservations or disagreements: "Each Party undertakes not to develop, test, or deploy sea-based, air-based, space-based, or mobile land-based ABM systems or their components." The JDT was cabled to Washington the next day, with a notation that the text fulfilled the delegation's instructions by including "components for future ABM systems which are not fixed and land-based." (U.S. Del SALT 1056, Sept. 24, 1971; the notation cited in Sofaer, *Cong. Rec.*, May 19, 1987, p. S6629.)[10]

At the time, no question was raised in the U.S. delegation or in Washington that the new text agreed upon in mid-September fulfilled the U.S. desire to ban development, testing, and deployment of mobile ABM systems and components. Later, however, in the course of carefully reviewing all parts of the text to be sure they carried out the desired purposes, the delegation itself in January 1972 saw a possible loophole in the language that was brought to Washington's attention and debated there.

On March 23, 1972, National Security Decision Memorandum

10. Sofaer argues that the U.S. delegation's reporting cable "misstated Karpov's language by describing the Soviets as having agreed that the text of Soviet Article V(1) included 'components for future ABM systems . . .'; according to the memcon [A-503] he agreed only that the language would extend to 'future components' of ABM systems." (Sofaer, *Cong. Rec.*, May 19, 1987, p. S6629; emphasis in original.) While there is a variation in the paraphrase, contrary to Sofaer's contention it was not substantive. If it had been, Karpov's acceptance of the phrase "future *components* of ABM systems" is not less inclusive, as Sofaer implies by saying he agreed "only" to that language, but *more* inclusive, since it would cover not only future systems but also systems that embodied even a single "future" component. In fact, at a later point the U.S. delegation proposed and the Soviet delegation accepted a change in the language to clarify this point, as noted in text to follow. Sofaer could therefore hardly have been unaware that the inference he was attempting to draw from this distinction was invalid.

158 directed the delegation to seek modification of Article V(1) to deal with the possible loophole that might have allowed development, testing, and deployment of a mobile ABM *component,* whether current or future technology, if such a mobile component was part of a fixed land-based ABM *system.* The language that the delegation was instructed to seek was presented to the Soviet delegation verbatim on April 5 and characterized as a "slight rewording" of the paragraph for the sake of greater clarity. The purpose of the change was made clear, and the Soviet delegation on April 10 accepted the American language. (See A-812, Apr. 5, 1972; A-813, Apr. 6, 1972; and A-840, Apr. 10, 1972.) Article V(1) assumed the wording that it had when the treaty was signed and has today: "Each Party undertakes not to develop, test, or deploy ABM systems or components which are sea-based, air-based, space-based, or mobile land-based."[11]

Subsequent Soviet references during the negotiation to Article V(1) covering future systems have been distorted or suppressed by Sofaer. For example, on December 4, in arguing against the need for the further U.S.-proposed provision on future systems, Vadim Chulitsky of the Soviet delegation stated that "the prohibition on air-based, [mobile] land-based, etc. ABM systems is adequate to cover the problem of future systems." (A-613, Dec. 4, 1971.) Sofaer lamely suggests this statement was "consistent with

11. Sofaer's interpretation stumbles on this issue by having to argue that Article V(1) never covered future systems, and that the U.S. delegation somehow failed to take up new instructions in April that he misreads as reflecting a perceived need for some further change in the text. Sofaer does not even raise this entire matter of the March–April revision in his unclassified report of May 11, 1987, having apparently abandoned it. The Sofaer argument from his classified August 1986 report, and its refutation, are presented in detail by Senator Nunn in his declassified report of May 19, 1987, reprinted in the *Congressional Record.* See Nunn, *Cong. Rec.,* May 20, 1987, pp. S6818–20.

Some of the relevant documents in the negotiating record that were not included in Sofaer's reports bear directly on this point. The minor revision of Article V(1) and three other articles was first brought up with the Soviet delegation by me on April 5 (A-812), and then formally by Parsons on April 6 (A-813); Grinevsky noted on April 8 that it would be accepted (A-825), and on April 10 it was (A-840). The details of this fuller record further underscore Nunn's point that this change was treated throughout by both sides as one of a number of minor editorial changes.

the position that the Soviets had agreed to regulate future 'components' consisting of missiles, launchers, and radars, but not unknown devices." (Sofaer, *Cong. Rec.*, May 19, 1987, p. S6633.) That is sheer inventive speculation and projection of Sofaer's own preferred interpretation onto a statement that both on its face and in its context clearly conveys the opposite. In fact, Chulitsky specifically said he was talking about "unknown" systems, and that "no one knew what future systems might be." And on no occasion did any Soviet source ever mention the idea of "future" versions of current components; that is entirely Sofaer's imaginative, if unpersuasive, vehicle for attempting to rewrite the history of the negotiation.

In another case, Academician Aleksandr Shchukin on November 30, just after the delegations had returned from a two-month recess, described the September agreement on Article V(1) as "of fundamental importance," and said that the Soviet acceptance of the U.S. position had been "confirmed in Moscow" during the recess. (A-594, Nov. 30, 1971.) Sofaer simply ignores this important reference rather than even attempt to explain it away.

There was subsequently little discussion of Article V(1), as Sofaer remarks, but that was true of all articles on which agreement had been reached. The delegations were too busy with those matters on which agreement had not yet been reached.

Agreement on Article V(1) in mid-September 1971 had left unagreed the second U.S. draft provision (originally 6(1)), which banned deployment of future fixed land-based ABM systems or components based on other physical principles. That matter remained unresolved until February 2, 1972. Before reviewing that issue, however, it is appropriate to turn to an issue that affects the significance of the agreement on Article V(1), namely the question of identifying or defining ABM system components. If components were defined as *only* ABM launchers, interceptor missiles, and radars, then notwithstanding the intention of both parties in September to agree on a ban on development and testing of all possible mobile ABM systems and components, they would not yet have done so.

Definition of ABM Components

Beginning with its submission of a draft treaty on July 27, the U.S. delegation sought *functional* definitions of ABM systems and components in Article II. The Soviet approach was to tie down the *descriptions* of ABM systems and components, with the result that successive versions of Soviet proposals on Article II circumscribed components by reference to ABM launchers, ABM interceptor missiles, and ABM radars. This language of course precluded a definition of components that would comprehend future ones based on other physical principles, although its purpose had been to concentrate on identifiable ABM components and not on components of air defense or other systems. It remained the Soviet position during many discussions from late July until December 20–21, 1971.

Sofaer challenges the interpretation that Article V(1) covers future systems by pointing out that at the time V(1) was agreed upon (in September 1971), Article II(1) was unresolved. He is not on sound ground in arguing that the Soviets did not agree to what they said they were agreeing to when they accepted Article V(1). He is, however, correct in noting that unless and until language for Article II was agreed upon that defined "components" more broadly than ABM launchers, interceptor missiles, and radars, the negotiators would not have given effect to the desired ban on future systems and components.

The U.S. delegation was aware of the need to have a definition of ABM components that was not restricted to the three types existing at that time. Until December 20–21 it had not proved possible to obtain Soviet agreement. But Sofaer's analysis of the reasons for the impasse on Article II is faulty because he addresses the issue solely in terms of his interpretation, omitting or glossing over contrary evidence.[12] In addition, he chooses to ignore the

12. A glaring example of Sofaer's tendentious approach is his treatment of a statement by Karpov on September 2, 1971, relating both to the Article II dispute

fact, well documented, that considerations having nothing to do with the question of constraining future ABM technologies were dominant in the debate over Article II. Above all, it was clear that the main Soviet concern was impingement on Soviet air defenses.[13]

As early as September 15 and 17, in conversations of the chief of the Soviet delegation, Vladimir Semenov, with myself and with Ambassador Gerard C. Smith, head of the U.S. delegation, the

---

and to the unresolved Article V issue on future systems. Sofaer states that "the components specified by the Soviets were limited on September 2 to the three presently in the Treaty, which Karpov announced were 'the means to which obligations should extend.' (A-540, Sept. 3, 1971, p. 1). This did not mean, Karpov stated, that other obligations did not exist in the Treaty 'which will cover other systems'." (Sofaer, *Cong. Rec.,* May 19, 1987, p. S6631.) Karpov was replying to a question from Graybeal whether under the Soviet approach the obligations of the treaty would apply only to the systems listed in Article II. What he said was not merely the words above quoted by Sofaer, but this: "Karpov replied that the 'fundamental basic obligations which deal with numerical limitations in the Soviet Article III [on permitted, limited deployments of current ABM system components] would be applied to these systems. It does not mean that there would not be other obligations listed in the treaty which would cover other systems.' " (Nunn, *Cong. Rec.,* May 20, 1987, p. S6813.) Thus he correctly related numerical (quantitative) obligations on current components to Article III. Moreover, he went on to mention as one of these other obligations that would be covered *elsewhere* in the treaty "Soviet Article V, which corresponds to paragraphs 2 and 3 of U.S. Article 6"—that is, *specifically* including the article on mobile systems, then U.S. 6(2), soon to be agreed as Article V(1).

Both in his classified memo of August 1986 and his report of May 11, 1987, Sofaer grudgingly concedes that this statement "provides limited support for the position that the Soviets would have accepted regulation of any ABM system with substitute devices for the usual components." (Sofaer, *Cong. Rec.,* May 19, 1987, p. S6631.) As Nunn notes, "However, he makes this concession almost in passing and never reconciles it with his basic thesis that the Soviets never agreed to include exotics under the coverage of Article V." (Nunn, *Cong. Rec.,* May 20, 1987, p. S6813.)

13. Senator Nunn, for example, without benefit of participation in the negotiation, had no difficulty in seeing even in the portions of the negotiating record provided on a classified basis to the Senate that Soviet concern over air defenses was "a principal reason" for Soviet caution and concern over Article II definitions, as well as the U.S. proposals on "other devices." Yet, as Nunn notes, "Surprisingly, the words 'air defense' do not appear anywhere in Sofaer's memo . . . despite the crucial role that the issue of air defenses played in the overall context of these discussions." (Nunn, *Cong. Rec.,* May 20, 1987, p. S6813.) Nunn is here referring to Sofaer's classified memorandum of August 12, 1986; the point is equally applicable to his report of May 11, 1987.

idea was raised of finding a "neutral" solution to Article II that did not prejudge substantive differences over other issues including the U.S.-proposed article on future fixed land-based systems (originally 6(1), now a bracketed V(3) in the JDT). I proposed the possibility to Semenov on September 15 in response to his request for assistance in finding an area where progress could be made. He then raised the matter two days later with Smith. He also commented to Smith that "he would be very reluctant to leave Article 2 in brackets. This would create an undesirable impression when he reported to his leadership upon coming home." (A-515, Sept. 15, 1971; and A-518, Sept. 17, 1971.) Nonetheless, no agreement was reached in the few days before a recess on September 24.

The next session resumed on November 15; it was approaching a pre-Christmas close before the issue was finally resolved. Again, as I was aware, Semenov was eager to resolve Article II to show progress.

On December 9, Soviet delegate Oleg Grinevsky made a very interesting presentation on Article II in a new small ad hoc negotiating forum called "the Four" (Grinevsky, Kishilov, Ambassador Parsons, and myself) that dealt with many issues on behalf of the delegations. He went through a presentation, I felt, "for the record"—highly unusual for the businesslike dealings in the Four. I noted this indirectly in the memcon by saying: "Grinevsky began by delivering a short speech to the effect that the Soviet side did not regard the article as necessary, that it had been found troublesome, and that it was something of a concession by his side even to be making the effort to resolve differences [on it]." He then conceded that "moreover, it was related to the differences contained in Article V" (at the time only V(3) was unagreed). I paraphrased and characterized his next points by writing: "His remarks implied that *members of his Delegation believed* there should be a 'tradeoff' involving the U.S. dropping Para 3 of Article V in exchange for Soviet acceptance of a definitional Article II as proposed by the U.S. side." (A-633, Dec. 9, 1971; emphasis added.)

I was sure that what this meant was that, indeed, some members of the Soviet delegation (I believed I knew which ones) wished to reject our proposal for prohibiting deployment of future fixed land-based ABM components (Article V(3)), and hoped—perhaps even knew—that there were members of the U.S. delegation and others in Washington who also were unenthusiastic about that constraint. So they pressed Semenov and Grinevsky from the Foreign Ministry to propose a tradeoff that would render harmless Article II as a threat to their interest in land-based lasers by simultaneously gaining American withdrawal of its proposal for Article V(3). If Semenov and Grinevsky had believed there should and could be such a tradeoff, it would never have been advanced as an indirect indication that "some members" of their delegation "believed" there "should be" such a tradeoff. Moreover, they undoubtedly anticipated (correctly) that I would reject the idea flatly and reaffirm the importance attached by the United States to the Article V(3) ban.

Not all these points would be clear to most readers of the memcon. (Incidentally, this is a good example of why it is useful to consult negotiators to assist in interpreting negotiating history.) But in any case the reader of Judge Sofaer's classified memorandum and published report is spared the need for pondering the meaning of this evidence, because he omits the entire first sentence cited above, and when citing the last sentence he deletes and substitutes ellipses for the italicized passage referring to "members" of the Soviet delegation "believing" in the possibility. Thus he leaves the uncomplicated picture of a Soviet proposal that "there should be a tradeoff."

Sofaer also presumably misunderstands, and certainly misrepresents, my response. He does cite the key operative sentence: "Garthoff stated again that the U.S. side considered Article II to be important, that the definitional approach was non-prejudicial to Soviet as well as American positions on other articles such as Article V, and that the U.S. position on Article V involved a matter of important substance which could not be 'traded.' " But the only thing Sofaer sees in that statement is that "the U.S. reply sought to reassure the Soviets that a definitional approach in Article II would not be prejudicial as to the content of Article V(3)." (Sofaer, *Cong. Rec.*, May 19, 1987, S6632.)[14] That was *one* element of what

14. Sofaer makes a revealing slip in identifying, correctly, Article V(3) as the

I said. But Sofaer ignores the clear message that there could not be a trade for Article V(3). As the review of later developments will show, this step did help to dispose of Soviet objections and permit agreement on the American position on Article II, as well as putting the necessary solid foundation under Article V(1).

Sofaer also ignores the remainder of the memcon. In replying to Grinevsky, I went on to state that while the United States was not "proposing any particular 'package,'" Grinevsky and Kishilov of course recognized that we were working simultaneously on possible resolution of differences on a number of articles, and had to find some combination of such articles which would represent in the eyes of both Delegations an equitable balance of movement on various points by both sides; we considered that Article II should be included in such a group of articles. Articles V and VI, on the other hand, like Article III, evidently were not ripe for resolution at this time." (A-633, Dec. 9, 1971.)

In other words, I was rejecting a tradeoff of Article V(3) for II, and confirming that we would stand firm on Article V(3) for later resolution, but also that we were prepared to "deal" with some package that included Soviet acceptance of Article II.[15]

"Grinevsky nodded understanding," the memcon continues, "and remarked that his side would *need* to address Articles II and V on some early occasion, *but* that our *informal work* on resolving differences *should continue and would be the best way to reach agreement*." In other words, they would repeat their old position on Article II for the record, but we could continue our informal negotiation and probably find a suitable package. As I further reported in the memcon, but Sofaer omits from his account, "In these comments, Grinevsky seemed to imply that it would be

---

provision that would not be prejudiced. According to his whole line of argument, the Soviets were still trying to protect V(1) on mobile future systems, which—if their position had been as Sofaer attributes it—*would* have been prejudiced by accepting the American definitional approach to Article II.

15. I did not state what such a trade might involve from the U.S. side. What I had in mind was Article I(2), a Soviet proposal in which they were very interested, and on which the U.S. side had been reserved. I referred to a possible package in order to signal interest in moving ahead on Article II, where I believed the Soviets were preparing to give in. Agreement on Article II, and on Article I, was reached on December 21, as described in the text following.

necessary for his delegation to go through a ritual of trying to get concessions from our side on Article V before he would be authorized to reach an agreement accepting the basic U.S. position on Article II." (A-633, Dec. 9, 1971; emphasis added.)

A breakthrough came on December 20 and 21, in three long meetings of "the Four." Several aspects of the ABM treaty negotiation were settled, including the key issue in Article II. Responding to a new U.S. draft article that I had given to Grinevsky earlier in the day, he noted the absence of a "connective" between the definition of ABM systems and the three subparagraphs identifying ABM components: launchers, interceptor missiles, and radars. He suggested "namely," or "consisting of." I countersuggested the phrase "currently consisting of," a new idea, and Grinevsky and Kishilov seemed uncertain as to what the Soviet reaction would be. I did not attempt to gloss over the effect of such language; it would mean that "components" would *not* be restricted to the familiar three that were then "current." On the contrary, I argued that "the Soviet side, as well as the American, recognized that there could be *future* systems, and while the question of constraints on future systems would be settled elsewhere than in Article II, the correct way of indicating a valid connection between components and systems in Article II would be to include the word 'currently.' " (A-677, Dec. 20, 1971.) Grinevsky agreed to take up that proposal with his delegation, and the next day brought a new Soviet draft of Article II incorporating that language and providing the basis for agreement on the article as a whole. (A-678, Dec. 21, 1971.) A fully agreed upon Article II was incorporated into the latest version of the Joint Draft Text of the treaty compiled the next day, December 22, and sent to Washington. Article II, and the coverage of mobile ABM components based on future technologies in Article V(1), were now in place.

In his report and in his earlier classified memorandum, Sofaer omits a key portion of the record. As Senator Nunn has disclosed in his declassified report:

The memcon of the December 21 meeting reveals that in accepting the U.S. proposal, Grinevsky and Kishilov emphasized "a very delicate situation within the Soviet Delegation" wherein "the expression 'currently consisting of' had been strongly objected to by some members of the Soviet delegation." The members in question were presumably the Soviet military. In short, the two Soviet negotiators were revealing that it had taken a struggle to gain approval for Garthoff's proposal. Sofaer does not explain why there would have been such a fight within the Soviet delegation if, as he believes, Garthoff's language did not have the effect of bringing future systems under the definition of "ABM system" in Article II. Indeed, Sofaer fails even to note that Grinevsky and Kishilov revealed this information. (Nunn, *Cong. Rec.*, May 20, 1987, pp. S6820–21.)[16]

In accepting Article II the Soviet delegation was well aware of what it was doing: it was agreeing to a functional definition that covered future mobile systems. The agreement cannot be reconciled with Sofaer's interpretation of Article V(1), but it is fully compatible with the other clear signs that the Soviets knowingly accepted the idea of banning development and testing of future mobile components and systems. The still-unresolved issue of a ban on deployment of future fixed land-based components was not prejudiced by the Soviet action on Article II, and it was this difference to which I had referred on December 20.

Sofaer has had to distort the plain meaning of Article II, trying to turn the illustrative identification of then-current components (that is, missiles, launchers, and radars) into a limiting definition. He has similar difficulty in dealing with the negotiating record, especially now that a large part of it has been made public. In his *Harvard Law Review* article published in June 1986, in which he overconfidently assumed that the actual texts from the negotiating record would remain classified,[17] he claimed in flat contradiction to the subsequently disclosed record that "the negotiating record

16. Sofaer also deleted this portion of the memcon (A-678) from the declassified version appended to his May 11, 1987, report.

17. Sofaer led off his discussion of the negotiating record in the *Harvard Law Review* with the statement that "the negotiating record of the ABM Treaty—like that of virtually all treaties—is classified. Details of the negotiations therefore cannot be revealed." (*Harvard Law Review* [June 1986], p. 1978.) The matter of

also contains strong support for a reading of Article II(1) that restricts the definition of 'ABM system' and 'components' to systems and components based on then-utilized physical principles. The Soviets specifically sought to prevent broader definitions of these terms, and the United States negotiators acceded to their wishes."[18]

In his August 1986 classified memorandum and his May 1987 report, with the record in large part provided to the Senate, Sofaer has had to rely more on misrepresentation and distortion, rather than suppression and misstatement, of the record. He now claims that the Soviet delegation accepted the language of Article II "only after Garthoff assured them that 'the question of constraints on future systems would be settled elsewhere than in Article II' " *and* "after Garthoff and the U.S. Delegation had implemented this assurance by agreeing to drop Article V(3) of the U.S. draft and to seek instead a separate, agreed minute to the Treaty on the subject of future devices." (Sofaer, *Cong. Rec.*, May 19, 1987, p. S6632.)[19] This explanation is both untrue and absurd on its face.

The Soviets did not seek and I did not give any "assurance" as a quid pro quo, or indeed at all. I took advantage of a Soviet suggestion for a connective to propose language that would meet our objective in a way that might be acceptable to the Soviet side. I took the initiative in noting its direct relevance to the future-systems issue, and in noting (not "assuring") that the matter of *constraints* would be settled elsewhere—having in mind Articles I, III, IV, V, and perhaps others and associated agreed interpreta-

---

disclosing the negotiating record is a separate issue and will be discussed later. But note Sofaer's confidence that the record could be kept from public—and congressional—inquiry. It was only in August 1986 that the administration agreed to provide relevant portions of the record to key senators under strict safeguards, and only in May 1987 that it was decided (over Sofaer's objection) to declassify and release his report and excerpts from the negotiating record.

18. Ibid., p. 1979.

19. Curiously, this language goes even beyond the otherwise identical text in his classified memo of August 1986, by substituting the words "had implemented this assurance" for "made this assurance tangibly credible" in describing the second of these alleged elements of a quid pro quo. (See Nunn, *Cong. Rec.*, May 20, 1987, p. S6821.)

tions. These included Article V(1), already agreed upon; Article I, on which we also agreed on December 20–21 (about which more later); and Article V(3) or an agreed interpretive statement, on which negotiation was still under way. It was indeed the case that the idea of an agreed interpretation also was actively being discussed in the December 20–21 meetings along with about a dozen other issues. But Sofaer implies a direct connection. Writing of the U.S. suggestion of possibly replacing proposed Article V(3) (banning deployment of fixed land-based ABM systems or components based on future technologies) with a separate agreed minute to the treaty, Sofaer states: "Garthoff's suggestion was made on December 20" and "a U.S. proposal . . . was tabled on December 21, the day on which the Soviets agreed to add 'currently consisting of' to paragraph 1 of Article II." (Sofaer, ibid.) That is, Sofaer tries to support his inference by suggesting that I presented the idea for an agreed minute on future-system constraints *in tandem with* the proposed new text for Article II on December 20, and that Soviet acceptance on December 21 was *in conjunction with* a further U.S. assurance and agreement to drop Article V(3).

But the record contradicts his inference. In the first place, I had initially proposed a possible agreed minute on December 17, not December 20, and not in conjunction with discussion of Article II. (A-663 and A-667, Dec. 17, 1971.) In fact, it stemmed from discussions in the U.S. delegation given impetus by a conversation of Academician Shchukin with Paul Nitze on December 14, also not related to Article II. (A-647, Dec. 14, 1971.) Moreover, the U.S. proposal for an agreed minute was clearly stated to be a procedural proposal while "maintaining our basic position on this matter," and any relinquishment of Article V(3) was made contingent on "a clear agreed understanding as part of the negotiating record." Indeed, the U.S. delegation did not give up its draft Article V(3) until February 2, 1972, when we received final Soviet assent to Agreed Statement D—but the Soviet delegation accepted Article II(1), with no "brackets" of reservation, on December 21, 1971. The Sofaer interpretation on Article II falls of its own weight.[20]

20. In addition, Sofaer cites two later Soviet statements in the negotiation and one comment of an American negotiator that he argues support an inference

Later in the negotiation, on January 31, Grinevsky and Kishilov argued against a U.S.-proposed formulation for an agreed statement dealing with future systems on the grounds it lacked a specific reference to ABM systems. They stressed that since Article II included reference to ABM systems and components, the agreed statement should do so as well. (A-763, Jan. 31, 1972.) This Soviet initiative in connecting Article II to future systems and to the Agreed Statement (D) sharply contradicts Sofaer's reinterpretation scheme. He makes no reference to it.

The Ban on Defense of the Territory of the Country

Debate on the reinterpretation issue has not to date given attention to the effect of Article I(2): "Each Party undertakes not to deploy ABM systems for a defense of the territory of its country and not to provide a base for such a defense, and not to deploy ABM systems for defense of an individual region except as provided for in Article III of this Treaty." To include it does not, of course, suit Sofaer's thesis that no part of the treaty itself deals with future technologies. Moreover, it was not an American proposal and not part of the U.S. strategy for dealing with future technologies.[21]

The United States had originally proposed on July 27 an anodyne Article I, essentially introducing the treaty. The Soviets accepted it on August 31.

During a recess in late September to mid-November the Soviet leadership reviewed, among other things, the U.S. proposal for banning deployment of fixed land-based ABM systems based on future technologies. After its return, the Soviet delegation on November 19 made an unexpected move. It proposed reopening

---

that Article II did not relate to future systems. Senator Nunn has dealt with these in detail, and I can simply cite here and endorse his conclusion: "The negotiating record reveals that none of the three statements substantiate his argument." (Nunn, ibid., and see pp. S6821–22.)

21. Hence the negotiating record provided in the Sofaer and Nunn reports deals only tangentially with Article I. Accordingly, the relevant events are summarized here for the first time.

the agreed text of Article I to add a new provision banning deployment by each side of ABM systems for defense of the territory of its country.

The U.S. delegation was leery of this new proposal, and some members were concerned that the Soviet side might seek to substitute the generality of their new Article I for more specific U.S. proposals tightly limiting ABM components, restricting non-ABM radars, guarding against upgrading air defenses, and banning deployment of fixed land-based ABM systems based on future technologies. The delegation advised Washington (on December 2) that it would inform the Soviet delegation that such a broad undertaking was no substitute for specific provisions implementing those broad objectives. Meanwhile, discussion on all proposed provisions continued.

On November 30, Kishilov told me that the Soviets regarded their new Article I as a partial substitute for the American-proposed Article V(3) on future technologies. On December 2, I told Kishilov that their new Article I was no substitute for the U.S.-proposed Article V(3). Again on December 10, Academician Shchukin argued to Nitze and Brown that the Soviet-proposed Article I "would ban the deployment of future systems in a manner providing a territorial defense," an objective with which he expressed no disagreement. (A-592, Nov. 30, 1971; A-600, Dec. 2, 1971; and A-639, Dec. 10, 1971.)

Meanwhile, from December 7 to 20 negotiation on the language of the Soviet draft Article I subparagraph was under way, converting it into something the U.S. delegation believed could be a useful reinforcement of other provisions by banning not only a nationwide defense but also a base for such a defense and reinforcing the tight, specific regional deployment constraints we were seeking in Article III.

December 20 and 21 saw intensive negotiations on Article I successfully concluded. On December 20, Grinevsky proffered a Soviet proposal building on the discussions we had been having since I had given him a counterdraft on December 7. It omitted one element that the U.S. delegation considered important and that I therefore urged be added (the clause "and not to provide the base for such a defense" [of the territory of the country]). Grinevsky agreed to seek its inclusion, and on December 21 reported his delegation's acceptance. Article I was now agreed, with the new provision as Article I(2). (A-678, Dec. 21, 1971; deleted from Sofaer's excerpt version of this memcon.)

On December 2 I had rejected the Soviet-proposed Article I as a substitute for the U.S.-proposed Article V(3), and on December 10 Nitze had pursued a suggestion by Shchukin on a provision involving consultation and agreement through the Standing Commission to deal with V(3). But on neither of these occasions had the U.S. side rejected the Soviet argument that their proposed ban on defense of national territories in Article I was relevant to banning systems based on future technologies capable of providing a nationwide defense against strategic ballistic missiles. (A-600, Dec. 2, 1971; and A-639, Dec. 10, 1971.) Moreover, on December 21, when I presented Grinevsky with the official U.S. delegation proposal for an agreed statement that could serve in place of Article V(3), that initial U.S. draft *incorporated* reference to Articles I and III as embodying deployment limitations that both parties agreed not to be circumvented by using "other" (future) ABM system components. (A-678, Dec. 21, 1971.) Later we dropped the reference to Article I when the statement was redrafted to read that both parties agreed not to deploy except as *allowed* in Article III, because it was then no longer appropriate.

At a later stage in the negotiation, in April 1972, I presented Grinevsky with the U.S. interpretation of the key phrase of Article I(2) banning deployment of ABM systems for a defense of the territory of its country as referring to ABM deployments that would provide defense covering substantially the whole of the contiguous territory of each country. A week later, Grinevsky reported that the Soviet delegation did not disagree with that formulation. We then agreed that a formal interpretive statement (such as Agreed Statement D and others) was unnecessary. While this discussion did not explicitly deal with future systems, it did carry implications for any type of system capable of providing nationwide, as opposed to regional, defensive coverage. (A-812, Apr. 5, 1972; and A-847, Apr. 13, 1972.)

All of these discussions were, of course, fully reported, and there were no objections within the delegation or from Washington. Since the operative language of Article I(2) refers to "ABM systems," defined in Article II to include components not limited to the then-current ones, Article I(2) clearly includes future systems based on other physical principles.

Sofaer omits *all* of this negotiating history in his classified 1986 and declassified 1987 reports. Moreover, none of the relevant documents from the negotiating history was included in the classified material made available to the Senate, except for the incidental inclusion for other reasons of the memoranda of the December 21 Garthoff-Grinevsky and December 10 Brown-Nitze-Shchukin discussions.[22]

The Ban on Deployment of Future Fixed Land-Based ABM Systems and Components

Agreement on the ban on mobile ABM systems and components, including those based on future technologies, in Article V(1) in mid-September (tied down by agreement on the definitional Article II in December) left unresolved the other provision on fixed, land-based systems called for in the August instructions to the U.S. delegation and incorporated in draft Article 6(1), after September 17 denominated draft Article V(3). Sofaer asserts that the Soviets' continuing objection to this second provision is evidence they had never really agreed to ban future mobile systems and components. Thus he argues, "Additional proof that the Soviets had not accepted the regulation of 'other devices' in U.S. Article 6(2) [V(1)] is the fact of their continued opposition on September 15 to Article 6(1)

22. In this instance, Sofaer and his researchers may simply have been unaware of the relevance of Article I(2) and its negotiating history, although it is all in the record, in part even in some memoranda he cites. It also could easily have been called to his attention if he had consulted more than one of the negotiators.

The materials were not provided to the Senate because the Senate had been able to couch its request only in terms of materials concerning portions of the record it had identified as relevant from Sofaer's 1985 testimony, that is, Articles II, III, V, and Agreed Statement D.

of the U.S. draft, which also referred to unknown 'other devices'."
(Sofaer, *Cong. Rec.,* May 19, 1987, p. S6630.) He assumes that
"had the Soviets agreed to prohibit development, testing, and
deployment of all future, unknown mobile 'devices' that could
replace known systems or components, they *should* have been far
more accommodating in accepting Article 6(1)," presumably because it banned only deployment. (Ibid.; emphasis added.) Sofaer
has substituted *his* assumptions about what the Soviets "should"
have done for the record of what they actually did. His logic,
moreover, is flawed. Months earlier the Soviets had themselves
proposed banning the testing as well as deployment of mobile
systems, while not proposing to ban all fixed land-based deployment of current systems, so why assume some other explanation
was needed when future systems were involved?

The real interest of both Soviet and American military and
technical specialists in future systems in 1971–72 was focused on
fixed land-based, in particular laser, systems. That is why the *U.S.*
position differentiated in its treatment of the two. The NSDM 127
instruction to the U.S. delegation, and the U.S. draft treaty
provisions 6(1) and 6(2), *intentionally avoided* any explicit reference to fixed land-based systems, but the secret NSDM specified
that these provisions "should not prohibit the development and
testing of future ABM components in a fixed, land-based mode."[23]

The treaty ratification proceedings will be discussed later, but it
is useful in the present connection to cite a statement by General
Bruce Palmer, Jr., acting chief of staff of the U.S. Army, in the
Senate 1972 ratification hearings, explaining why the treaty allowed
development of fixed, land-based ABM systems only and banned
development and testing of mobile systems. He stated, on the
subject of future systems: "On the question of the ABM, the facts
are that when the negotiation started the only system actually
under development, in any meaningful sense, was a fixed, land-
based system." And he declared, in response to sharp probing by
Senator Henry M. Jackson, that the Joint Chiefs of Staff went
along with "a concept that does not prohibit the development in

23. NSDM 127, August 12, 1971; cited in Sofaer, *Cong. Rec.,* May 19, 1987,
p. S6627.

the fixed, land-based ABM system. We can look at futuristic systems as long as they are fixed and land-based."[24]

In short, the relevant point was not—as Sofaer argues—that both paragraphs of the U.S. proposal dealt with unknown, future systems; it was that the Soviets were quite prepared early on to ban deployment and even testing of all mobile systems and components but were evidently divided over banning deployment of future components for fixed land-based systems. It therefore took some time before they agreed to the latter. As Shchukin put it plainly to Harold Brown and Paul Nitze, although they agreed on the objective of banning "the deployment of future systems in a manner providing a territorial defense," including all mobile systems, if future components could carry out the same tasks as allowed (fixed, land-based) components "in a more efficient and less costly manner," why prohibit them? (A-639, Dec. 10, 1971.)

Sofaer rests much of his argument, not on what is *stated* in the negotiating record, but on what is unsaid—and what he infers from that absence. For instance he repeatedly stresses his view that from mid-September through January neither delegation, in discussing the American-proposed ban on deployment of future fixed land-based systems (Article 6(1), then Article V(3), then an agreed minute, eventually Agreed Statement D), must have been referring to future systems in general, in all basing modes, because they did not refer *specifically* to fixed land-based systems and components. Thus the Soviets often objected to an attempt to deal with "unknown, future" devices, without specifying that they were referring to fixed land-based systems. And the American negotiators kept urging a provision to ban deployment of systems based on future technologies without specifying they were referring to fixed land-based systems. This is perhaps the strongest element in Sofaer's line of argument, because he does not need to explain away statements that do not fit his interpretation, and because the reason for the lack of specificity is not immediately evident. The

24. *Military Implications of the Treaty on the Limitations of Anti-Ballistic Missile Systems and the Interim Agreement on Limitation of Strategic Offensive Arms,* Hearing before the Senate Committee on Armed Services, 92 Cong. 2 sess. (Government Printing Office, 1972), p. 443.

basic reason is that the language of the U.S. proposal did not use those words, and by design.

The U.S. delegation did not refer explicitly to fixed land-based systems because, in accordance with its instructions, it did not wish to draw attention to U.S. interest in future land-based lasers. If pressed on the reason for seeking to ban only deployment of future fixed land-based systems, while having sought and obtained agreement on banning development and testing of future mobile systems as well, that interest could be revealed.

The Soviets did not choose to focus their objections to dealing with "unknown, future" technology explicitly on fixed land-based systems for similar reasons. This would have opened them up to charges of inconsistency in having agreed to ban deployment of future mobile systems, and they were probably under instructions not to be explicit about the *Soviet* interest in fixed land-based laser systems.

Sofaer argues that if the U.S. delegation believed the Soviets had accepted the coverage of future mobile systems in Article V(1), it would have been "natural" to ask the Soviets "why they were so adamantly opposed to regulating such devices in Article V(3)." (Sofaer, *Cong. Rec.*, May 19, 1987, p. S6633.) The U.S. delegation did not talk explicitly about fixed land-based systems in the negotiation for the same reason it had not made explicit references to those systems in the proposed treaty provisions: the delegation's instructions had made clear it was not supposed to do so. Sofaer himself cites the text of NSDM 127 paragraphs 1 and 2 that were "translated" into draft treaty language by the delegation (and reviewed and approved in Washington before being presented to the Soviet delegation). In that NSDM text the only reference to fixed land-based systems was in the earlier-cited parenthetical sentence provided only for the delegation's background guidance. (See Sofaer, ibid., p. S6627.) Senator Nunn has revealed that in Sofaer's 1986 classified report to the Senate, he had even failed to disclose "a crucial portion" of the instructions, paragraph 5 of the NSDM. In his May 1987 declassified report, Sofaer has partially remedied that glaring omission, but he still deleted one key phrase (italicized): "*In presenting this position,* the Delegation should not

invite a detailed negotiation or discussion of future ABM systems."
(Compare Sofaer, *Cong. Rec.*, May 19, 1987, p. S6627, with Nunn,
Cong. Rec., May 20, 1987, p. S6813.) Senator Nunn comments:
"Paragraph 5 of NSDM 127 reflected the extreme sensitivity within
the U.S. Government about the dangers of revealing too much
information about highly-classified U.S. military research then
being conducted in such areas as lasers and particle-beam weapons." (Nunn, ibid.) He does not note the fact, but these were fixed
land-based systems.

As noted earlier, after a number of formal presentations of
argument and informal discussion from late November to late
December 1971, agreement was reached on December 21 to seek
an agreed interpretive statement as a possible alternative to a
subparagraph in Article V. Contrary to the picture presented by
Sofaer, this was not a simple story of "adamant," "profound,"
"sincere," and "principled" Soviet "rejection." Although the
Soviets voiced misgivings that such a provision was unnecessary,
imprecise, superfluous, and dealing with things not adequately
known, they did not flatly reject it. For example, shortly before the
recess in September, a month after the U.S. delegation had proposed the provisions covering future systems, the chief of the
Soviet delegation, Deputy Foreign Minister Semenov, told Ambassador Smith that with respect to the U.S. proposal on future
systems, which was a new issue, "naturally the Soviet side had
carefully listened to the considerations expressed in support of the
U.S. position," and "obviously this problem would be kept in his
field of vision during the preparations in Moscow" for the next
session. (A-518, Sept. 17, 1971.) Many statements in December
also suggested a desire to reach accommodation on the issue,
including use of some formula of consultation and agreement before
any deployment of future systems.

When the delegations resumed work in January 1972, besides
formal meetings at which the problem was addressed, the informal
negotiation intensified. Sofaer notes the formal sessions on January
11 and 14, 1972, at which the unresolved element of the future-
technology question was discussed. He also notes about half of the
twelve less-formal active negotiating sessions held from January

11 through February 2 in which Agreed Statement D was worked out and agreed upon. His treatment of this entire phase of the negotiation is, however, curiously incomplete, as well as seriously distorted.[25]

Sofaer cites two internal U.S. delegation drafts of a possible message (never sent) dated January 8 and 10 outlining the fact that agreed Articles I and II, and the U.S. version of Article III, could be read to ban any deployment of future ABM systems because they banned any deployment of ABM components except as allowed in Article III. The drafts considered the negotiating strategy of exploring with the Soviet delegation whether they, too, interpreted Articles I, II, and III as having this effect, and if so the possibility of doing without either a treaty provision or an agreed interpretive statement, relying instead "solely on interpretation of these articles." The delegation concluded, however, that it was preferable to have an agreed statement rather than "no explicit provision."[26]

On January 11, in a three-hour session of "the Four," I posed the issue of whether given Articles I, II, and III there was any right of deployment of future ABM systems, for example laser interceptors. Sofaer concedes that "these exchanges led Grinevsky and Kishilov individually to indicate that they regarded Articles I, II and III as together banning the deployment of future systems."

25. At least in 1985, Sofaer's knowledge of the negotiating history of Agreed Statement D was so weak that when he testified before the Senate Armed Services Committee on November 21, 1985, he contended that "more than anybody else in the record, Nitze played a crucial role in statement D," and "he agreed with my conclusions and I must say I was not too bashful to accept that as a reassuring factor." (*Strategic Defense Initiative*, Hearings before the Subcommittee on Strategic and Theater Nuclear Forces of the Senate Armed Services Committee, 99 Cong. 1 sess. [GPO, 1986], p. 184.) Ambassador Smith, later in the same hearing, refuting Sofaer in his interpretation, also noted that Agreed Statement D had been drafted not by Nitze but by Garthoff. (Ibid., p. 248.)

26. Sofaer completely distorts the meaning of the very drafts he cites, claiming that the second one "eliminated the thought of approaching the Soviets on the meaning of Article II alone." In fact, the January 8 draft contained no such proposal so there was nothing of the kind to be "eliminated" in the redraft. *Both* drafts concerned a strategy of interpretation of Articles I, II, and III together. This is clear from reading the very excerpts Sofaer himself cites. (See Sofaer, *Cong. Rec.*, May 19, 1987, pp. S6634–35.)

(Sofaer, *Cong. Rec.*, May 19, 1987, p. S6635.) Nonetheless, the discussion had revealed (in particular a side comment by Grinevsky to Parsons) that some members of the Soviet delegation, presumably military, might not hold that view. I therefore stressed to Grinevsky and Kishilov that "it was essential to establish a common understanding between the two Delegations with respect to the effect of Articles I, II, and III on future ABM systems, and to reach agreement on a position concerning this subject." And in an internal comment in the memcon I noted that some of the discussion seemed to "indicate absence of a clear and thought-through position on the part of the Soviet delegation at the present time" on this point. (A-710, Jan. 11, 1972.)

Sofaer miscites that comment (written by me as an aside in the reporting memorandum) as suggesting that "the U.S. delegation doubted that the Soviets in fact agreed with Garthoff's interpretation." (Sofaer, *Cong. Rec.*, May 19, 1987, p. S6635.) We did not "doubt" their understanding, but we were not certain that the Soviet delegation as a whole at that time understood and accepted— as Grinevsky and Kishilov did—that Articles I, II, and putatively III (the latter still not agreed) would ban deployment of futures. And we were determined to nail it down. We did not want any papering over if there was any disagreement or reservation—we wanted a clear understanding, preferably codified in a formal agreed interpretive statement. We saw no disadvantage in reinforcing redundancy.

Another point that had arisen needed immediate clarification. Grinevsky had commented that "the treaty referred to ABM systems, which were defined in Article II. It could not deal with unknown other systems." I rejoined by noting that "the treaty dealt not only with ABM systems comprising components identified in Article II, but all ABM systems," and that "the issue did not concern 'other' [that is, non-ABM] systems, but rather future ABM systems." Grinevsky understood, and did not challenge that view. Sofaer, however, either does not or chooses not to understand what we were talking about. He argues that "Garthoff's analysis [in this exchange with Grinevsky] might itself have contributed to the confusion. His attempted distinction between 'other' and

'future' ABM systems had nothing to do with his point that the
parties might disagree over whether something was an ABM
system. The parties were using the words 'other' and 'future'
interchangeably. . . .'' It is true that those words were sometimes
used interchangeably (particularly as we realized "future" *could*
be interpreted as excluding technologies such as lasers that were
"known" but not yet applied, so in the formal language we used
only "other physical principles" and components "capable of
substituting for"). What Sofaer fails to acknowledge is that the
term "other" systems was also being used to refer to air defense
and other non-ABM systems—and that a major part of the Soviet
concern was that the United States, while ostensibly limiting ABM
systems, by such language was seeking to impinge on such other
systems. In the given case, there is no question. In the sentence
immediately *preceding* the one with which Sofaer begins his
quotation of the exchange, Grinevsky had said " 'other' systems
might or might not be for ABM systems, but the U.S. wanted to
have a veto over them." (A-710, Jan. 11, 1972.) That is why I made
the distinction I did, and why Grinevsky accepted it and agreed
that Article II did cover future ABM systems.[27]

On January 14, in a similar exchange between Nitze and
Shchukin, who were also trying to tie down an understanding on
the combined effects of the other articles on future systems, when
Nitze referred to the restrictive effects of Article III in the light of
Article I, *Shchukin* had interjected the comment "and also in the
light of Article II." (A-713, Jan. 14, 1972.) This significant statement
by Academician Shchukin relating Article II to future systems,

27. See Sofaer, *Cong. Rec.,* May 19, 1987, p. S6635. Sofaer also asserts:
"Furthermore, Garthoff's arguments undercut the claimed need for an Agreed
Statement. If Articles I, II, and III together banned the deployment of all forms
of ABM systems, then a further provision doing so was unnecessary." (Ibid.)
Again, Sofaer appears so blinded by his own interpretation, that the only purpose
of Agreed Statement D was to cover future systems not covered anywhere else,
that he cannot even imagine that the delegation saw things quite differently. The
unsent draft he quoted earlier had made this very point. (Ibid., p. S6634.) The
U.S. delegation believed it essential to have a common understanding by the
Soviet delegation of the effect of all aspects of the treaty, in particular including
the synergistic effect of Articles I, II, and III on the deployment of future fixed
land-based systems, but it also believed there should be an explicit provision in
the form of an Agreed Statement.

directly contrary to Sofaer's thesis, is included in an excerpt given by Sofaer but goes unnoted in his text and ignored in his argument.

During mid-January the Soviets gradually moved from their initial position of seeking an agreed statement that would refer only to mutual consultation in the Standing Consultative Commission (in accordance with Article XIII) to acceptance of the U.S. insistence that any deployment of future land-based systems based on new technologies also be subject to mutual agreement and amendment (in accordance with Article XIV).[28]

There were also negotiating sessions on the subject on January 19 and 21 that Sofaer omits from the record, although they indicate the intensification of the effort and included a statement to me that the Soviet delegation was awaiting further instructions from Moscow that my interlocutors believed would permit agreement.

On January 26, in another meeting of the Four, the positions of the two sides came closer on the formulation of an agreed statement. Grinevsky objected to the need for a certain new formulation I proposed using the phrase "to perform the functions of" ABM launchers, interceptor missiles, and radars, on the grounds it raised again the question of non-ABM systems and was unnecessary. Sofaer reports this objection as though it were significant and says Grinevsky "adamantly opposed the change, making clear in the process that the Soviets remained committed to the view that the Agreed Statement covered future substitutes, and Article II covered the usual components." That is not only a misstatement, but it is all that Sofaer finds worth reporting in his three-sentence reference to the meeting of January 26. (Sofaer, *Cong. Rec.*, May 19, 1987, p. S6635.)[29]

---

28. Yet when for the first time the Soviet side offered a draft referring not only to Article XIII but also to Article XIV, clearly implying the need for agreement and amendment before any deployment, instead of seeing this as an important step toward the U.S. position Sofaer misleadingly comments that it "called *only* for discussion 'in accordance with Articles XIII and XIV . . .' " and adds, "The Soviets were still avoiding a clear commitment to agree on limitations before deployment." (Sofaer, *Cong. Rec.*, May 19, 1987, p. S6635.) Even where it is not germane to his interpretation, Sofaer seems unable to read the record straight, or at least to depict it accurately.

29. Perhaps it is just as well that Sofaer does not say more. He has dropped a statement made in his classified report of August 1986 claiming that in the

This meeting marked, in fact, a major step toward agreement, which was now close. Perhaps as important, rather than registering a discrepancy in U.S. and Soviet views and Soviet opposition, it was significant for some unusually clear-cut statements of agreement. First, Grinevsky's argument was not that my proposed new formulation advanced an unacceptable position, but that its language was superfluous and troublesome. As I recorded in my memcon, he pointed out that "the American side evidently had not considered such an addition necessary when it provided the earlier formulation, and the Soviet side did not consider it necessary. He noted that the sentence [without the proposed revision] *already makes clear* that reference is to *future ABM systems components other than the three* indicated in the sentence and in Article II of the treaty. Article II made clear that these are the three components *currently* comprising ABM systems, and the language under discussion [without the addition] made clear that it was referring to precisely such *system components other than the three current ones* that were listed." (A-743, Jan. 26, 1972; emphasis added.) Thus rather than taking the Sofaer interpretation on Article II, which Sofaer incorrectly projects and attributes to Grinevsky, Grinevsky in fact restated the U.S. position (or, rather, since December 21 the agreed U.S. and Soviet position).

Grinevsky had a point. On the spot, I agreed to seek approval for dropping the proposed addition, and Parsons and I agreed to seek U.S. delegation agreement to a new draft agreed statement—the first with no bracketed reservations (although at this stage ad referendum to delegations). (A-743, Jan. 26, 1972.) Why did Sofaer not find *these* points worth noting?

Nor is that all. In stressing the fact that the Soviet delegation had now accepted the last U.S. proposal, and there was no need for the addition, Grinevsky commented that the Soviet side "had

---

January 26 meeting "*both* Parties stated that Article II applied to three then-current components of ABM systems, and that Agreed Statement D would apply to all future components that would take the place of interceptors, launchers, or radars." (Cited by Nunn, *Cong. Rec.*, May 20, 1987, p. S6821.) As Nunn, with understatement, points out: "The negotiating record does not support Sofaer's description."

now *accepted the earlier American formulation completely,* and *in fact had accepted the American position on the subject entirely,* save only that it would be a jointly agreed interpretation rather than an article in the treaty." (A-743, Jan. 26, 1972; emphasis added.)

Why did Sofaer not find *that* statement worth reporting?

Over the next three days (January 27–29), four more meetings were held (two of the Four, one of myself with Grinevsky and Kishilov, and one of myself with Kishilov) carrying forward redrafting based on many specific suggestions from both delegations, focused largely on the wording of "system components" or "components" and the like. Sofaer makes no reference to three of these meetings and only a passing reference to the fourth. None is in the declassified memcons, and they were not even among the classified memoranda provided to the Senate. These excluded portions of the record show the continuing efforts of both sides to resolve the issues involved. The discussion also belies Sofaer's comments elsewhere alleging an earlier common usage of the term "components." Yet Sofaer has chosen not to review and disclose much of the negotiating record on Agreed Statement D, although it is the only element of the treaty that he regards as dealing with future systems.

On January 31 the negotiation entered the home stretch. In a meeting with Grinevsky and Kishilov, I began to read from talking points that had been carefully prepared by the delegation. This attracted attention because it was not my usual style. After making the points I therefore decided to give them the paper, in order to make crystal clear that they understood it. The five-point "Statement on 'Future ABM Systems' " summed up several matters on which the U.S. delegation wanted to ensure a common understanding in addition to working out an agreed statement. It nailed down the point that no ABM systems or components, as defined in Article II, could be deployed except as provided for in Article III, and that Article III (still under negotiation for other reasons) "should be drafted so as not to permit the deployment of devices other than ABM interceptor missiles, ABM launchers, or ABM radars to substitute for and perform their functions." It also clarified that "devices other than ABM interceptor missiles, ABM launchers, or ABM radars *could* be used as adjuncts to an ABM system provided that the devices could not perform the functions of and substitute for ABM interceptor missiles, ABM launchers, or ABM radars." As I reported, "After reading the talking points, Grinevsky said that he believed there was *complete agreement*." (A-763, Jan. 31, 1972; emphasis added.)

Sofaer's exegesis of the talking points is geared to supporting his own interpretation. He notes that the points all address only deployment. That, of course, had been true of *all* drafts of Article 6(1), Article V(3), and the Agreed Statement from the time we first proposed a provision August 17. Second, Sofaer notes that there was no reference to Article V(1) regulating future mobile systems. Quite true—there was no need to refer to a matter decided three and a half months earlier. Even Sofaer carefully notes that "the points were not expressly limited to land-based devices," but that was true of Article III as well, which Sofaer claims applies only to fixed land-based systems. (Sofaer, *Cong. Rec.*, May 19, 1987, p. S6636.) *Nowhere* in the treaty is there an explicit reference to fixed land-based systems.[30]

At the same January 31 meeting, I then presented a new and substantially revised draft agreed statement. The Soviet negotiators were dismayed that it involved substantial changes in language,

30. In criticizing Agreed Statement D for not referring explicitly to fixed land-based systems, and in arguing that the negotiating discussions did not do so either, Sofaer is trying to support his interpretation that they dealt also with mobile systems. But to do so he must not only ignore or distort the August–September negotiation on mobile systems in Article V(1), but also ignore that the delegation's instructions in August were framed to *avoid* explicit discussion of fixed land-based systems, and accordingly *all* U.S. proposals avoided such reference. Thus from the time of the very first U.S. proposals on future systems on August 17, Article 6(2) spoke explicitly of all the mobile-based systems, and 6(1) residually but *not* explicitly dealt with fixed land-based systems, which Sofaer himself grudgingly admits, saying at one point that 6(1) "presumably" dealt with "fixed land-based systems and components." (Sofaer, *Cong. Rec.*, May 19, 1987, p. S6627.)

Article III in its *specification* of allowed deployments deals only with fixed land-based components, but in its lead-in excluding *any* other ABM deployments, it deals with all types of fixed and mobile, current and future, ABM systems and components. See the discussion of Article III that follows.

and in particular that the U.S. delegation had now eliminated reference to "systems" and spoke only about "components."

Sofaer turns next to a meeting the following day and declares: "Grinevsky objected on February 1 to using Garthoff's five-point paper as a new text. He 'said that the Soviet Delegation had found interesting and helpful' the points given, but they thought the previous text should be used. . . ." (Sofaer, ibid.) No one, of course, had ever proposed using the five-point talking paper as a "new text," nor did most of it even address the agreed statement. Grinevsky did say that his delegation found the five points interesting and helpful, which is more important than Sofaer seems to recognize. And he reported that the Soviet delegation "did not see a need to move so drastically from the previous text" and did not think the latest proposed one was as good. During the discussion among the Four a number of suggestions were made, and I came up with a proposed solution that seemed acceptable to all. I sent a clean version of the proposal to the Soviet delegation, and after further telephonic exchanges the text was agreed upon. Because some members of the Soviet delegation were not immediately available, it was not until the next day that Kishilov informed me of its acceptance by the Soviet side. The U.S. delegation was fully in accord, and on February 2 the negotiation of Agreed Statement D was successfully concluded. (A-769, Feb. 1, 1972; and A-770, Feb. 2, 1972.) In April, a minor stylistic revision proposed by the U.S. delegation was accepted and the final language of Agreed Statement D settled. (A-838, Apr. 11, 1972.)

Article III: The Capstone

In April 1972 the negotiation began to come to grips with the last issues concerning the scope of the limited ABM deployments that would be allowed, as set out in draft Article III. At that juncture the U.S. delegation decided to nail down the last element in the interlocking net of provisions dealing with ABM systems and components based on future technology. Not only had the U.S. delegation long recognized the need to do so; we had made the point explicitly in late January in the final negotiation on Agreed Statement D.

On January 31, 1972, when I had given Grinevsky and Kishilov the five-point "Statement on 'Future ABM Systems' " referred to earlier, point four stated: "Article III should be drafted so as not to permit the deployment of devices other than ABM interceptor missiles, ABM launchers, or ABM radars to substitute for and perform their functions." (A-763, Jan. 31, 1972.) In referring to this in fleeting fashion, Sofaer misstates it and misrepresents the Soviet reaction, claiming that the paper said that "Article III should be drafted to prohibit *by implication* the deployment of 'future systems,' but the Soviets did not respond." (Sofaer, *Cong. Rec.,* May 19, 1987, p. S6637; emphasis added.) First, the American paper did not say the article should prohibit deployment of future systems "by implication" but flatly stated that Article III should be drafted "so as not to permit" such deployment. Second, the Soviet delegate, Grinevsky, after reading the paper, stated that he believed we were "in complete agreement." (A-763, Jan. 31, 1972.) Finally, the Soviet side promptly accepted the American proposal for a formulation of Article III that did just that.

On April 11 the U.S. delegation proffered lead-in language for Article III that clearly precluded any deployment of future technologies based on other physical principles. It accomplished this by explicitly exempting from a ban on deployment only specified numbers of the three then-current components: "Each Party undertakes not to deploy ABM systems or their components except that each Party may deploy ABM interceptor missiles, ABM launchers, and ABM radars within . . . " two specified circumscribed areas. (A-838, Apr. 11, 1972.) On April 26 I suggested to Grinevsky that an even more concise formulation would be simply: "Each Party undertakes not to deploy ABM systems or ABM components except as follows: . . . " (A-872, Apr. 26, 1972.) Two days later, Grinevsky said that the Soviet delegation could accept the more concise formulation "undertaking not to deploy ABM systems or their components except as the Article would provide." He also went on to observe that "this would ban 'other systems.' "

(A-873, Apr. 28, 1972.)[31] The final language was agreed without difficulty, and Article III begins: "Each Party undertakes not to deploy ABM systems or their components except that: . . . " (A-943, May 14, 1972.)

There was thus clear language and clear mutual understanding that Article III banned any deployment of other or future ABM components and systems. And the U.S. delegation so reported to Washington, referring to Soviet acceptance of the "US approach on lead-in [of Article III] *reinforcing* the interpretive statement [D] dealing with future ABM systems . . . ." (U.S. Del SALT 1289, May 6, 1972.)

Sofaer conceded in his classified report of August 1986 that this record "could be read as supporting the 'restrictive' interpretation," but he still purported to find that "doubtful." He attempts to explain these references by lamely suggesting that when Grinevsky had referred to the formulation as banning "other systems" he might have been referring to banning deployment of *current*-type ABM systems "at *locations* 'other than' those described in Article III," a far-fetched fantasy for which Sofaer can provide no foundation. (See Nunn, *Cong. Rec.,* May 20, 1987, p. S6822.)

Sofaer argues against the logic of Article III's application to future systems by claiming that such an interpretation would make Agreed Statement D "redundant," and *therefore* that must not have been the article's intent. This strained deductive argument is exposed as fallacious by the wording of Agreed Statement D itself, which is couched in terms of reinforcing III: "In order to *insure fulfillment* of *the obligation not to deploy* ABM systems and their components *except as provided in Article III. . . .* " And, as noted above, the delegation made this point in reporting agreement on Article III to Washington by observing that the language had the effect of "reinforcing" D. They were mutually supporting.

---

31. At this juncture, Ambassador Smith was in Washington, and I sent a cable to him on April 29 conveying the new formulation for such a lead-in that, I noted, would take care of the futures problem. Sofaer does not cite that document from the negotiating history nor did he make it available to the Senate.

Sofaer's argument about redundancy of D and III also fails to take into account that while D was agreed in January, Article III was not so formulated until May. As Senator Nunn notes, "In light of this chronology, the issue raised by the final agreement on Article III was not whether Agreed Statement D should be *added* to the Treaty, but whether this extremely complicated issue should be reopened by proposing to *delete* the agreed statement." (Nunn, ibid., p. S6823.) The delegation never even considered that course because we believed there was value in the two mutual reinforcing provisions, and so did the authorities in Washington.

Note also that Agreed Statement D performed another purpose. Significantly, it pointed out (although, in keeping with the delegation's instructions, implicitly) that if fixed land-based ABM components were created in the future, the parties had a channel for consultation and amendment to permit the limited deployment of such means in keeping with purposes of the treaty. The delegation thus saw D both as worthwhile in its own right and as fulfilling the delegation's instructions.

In an attempt to support his case, Sofaer also reviews the internal memoranda prepared by the U.S. delegation's legal adviser, John Rhinelander, from January through May of 1972. One of Rhinelander's purposes in those analyses was precisely to be a "devil's advocate"; that is, to question whether the delegation had, in fact, fully achieved its objectives and elicited clear Soviet concurrence. But Sofaer's methodology is seriously deficient. He cites portions of Rhinelander's analyses that suggest the delegation might need to make changes or reopen matters with the Soviet side, often misreads them, and then he ignores or suppresses the facts that show how the problems were taken care of. Those need not be reviewed here; Senator Nunn had access to the Rhinelander memoranda and has refuted Sofaer's misuse of them in detail.[32] Nunn also notes Sofaer's persistent "failure to note comments in

32. Rhinelander had published a careful analysis of the ABM Treaty in 1974 that made clear and explicit the agreed constraints on future systems. See John B. Rhinelander, "The SALT I Agreements," in Mason Willrich and John B. Rhinelander, eds., *SALT: The Moscow Agreements and Beyond* (The Free Press, 1974), pp. 125–59.

the analyses of the Treaty text prepared by the U.S. delegation's legal adviser that substantiate the Traditional Interpretation." (Nunn, ibid., p. S6824, and see ibid., pp. S6818–24.)

Sofaer also fails to cite another clear statement from the immediate postnegotiation record that refutes his claim that the U.S. delegation did not conceive of Article III as banning deployment of exotic future ABM systems, such as lasers. On June 16, 1972, on behalf of the U.S. SALT delegation, I briefed the permanent representatives of the North Atlantic Council in Brussels on the ABM Treaty and the SALT I Interim Agreement. This was the principal U.S. government briefing to the allies on the ABM Treaty, climaxing many consultations by Ambassador Smith and others of us during the negotiation from 1969 through 1972. In a special session with allied experts following the full council meeting, I was asked whether the deployment of laser interceptors was banned and replied that it was banned by Article III.[33]

Summing Up the Negotiating Record

The U.S. SALT I delegation set out in August 1971 to fulfill its new instructions to shape the treaty in such a way that it banned development, testing, and deployment of all mobile ABM systems and components, including future ones based on new physical principles, and deployment but not development or testing of fixed land-based systems based on new physical principles. Over the next nine months it did so, along with negotiating all the remaining provisions of the ABM Treaty.

While the delegation's tactics in the negotiation and draft treaty language naturally changed as new developments occurred (includ-

33. The U.S. Mission to NATO reporting cable has not been declassified, but there is no reason whatsoever that a pertinent excerpt from that message could not have been made available. Moreover, this document was not even included in the classified materials on the negotiating record or subsequent practice supplied to the U.S. Senate in August 1986 and May 1987.

In replying to the question,' I did not go into the difference in treatment of development and testing between mobile and fixed land-based systems, but noted that research was not banned.

ing new ideas on the American side, as well as interaction with the other negotiating party), its negotiating strategy was consistent: to build up gradually and cumulatively a network of interrelated and reciprocally reinforcing provisions in order to attain our objectives, including the handling of future ABM systems.

The record clearly shows that process at work. Article V(1) was agreed upon on September 15; Articles I(2) and II(1) were agreed upon on December 21; Agreed Statement D on February 1; and Article III on May 14. In addition, the nature of the constraints imposed by other related provisions were importantly affected, for example Article IV on permitted test ranges, and Article IX banning transfer of ABM systems or components, including blueprints, to any third country. Thus the negotiating record, just as the final text of the treaty, needs to be regarded as a whole. Its parts are mutually consistent and mutually reinforcing.

Judge Sofaer has adopted an entirely inadmissable approach based on an ulterior purpose. He has examined the treaty and its negotiation not to clarify the intent of the negotiators and the effect of the treaty language, but to look for any loopholes or alternate explanations that would free the hands of his client, the Reagan administration, for expanded SDI development and testing. He disaggregates the treaty and the record, and makes of the pieces a fictitious construct that serves his purpose, seeking to relegate all consideration of future ABM systems and components to Agreed Statement D alone. He has not hesitated not only to reinterpret, but to reorder, remove, and when necessary rewrite the record.

Sofaer's treatment of the negotiating record does not substantiate his case, even on the basis of those portions of the record he has provided. He attempts to explain away numerous points in the negotiating record that on their face clearly support the traditional interpretation. When necessary, he concedes a common-sense interpretation but attempts to downplay its significance by alleging other ways that evidence *could* be read to support his case. In other cases, however, Sofaer has simply not made the record available.[34]

34. Sofaer gradually expanded the portions of the record made available,

In some instances that might be attributable to ignorance of the record, though that is difficult to believe, and if true indicates incompetence. The only other explanation would be deliberate suppression of parts of the record. Why, for example, does Sofaer not report the unambiguous statement by the U.S. government representative to the North Atlantic Council in the culminating briefing for the allies in June 1972 that Article III of the treaty bans the deployment of laser interceptors—a specific illustration of the applicability of Article III (and by inference Article II) to a future ABM system component? Clearly because it contravenes Sofaer's whole thesis that only Agreed Statement D dealt at all with future ABM systems and components. Yet this datum was not made available to the Senate even on a classified basis. And this is but one example, although a telling one, of his practice.

---

even providing some in his unclassified report of May 11, 1987, that had not been included in the classified file provided to the Senate in August 1986. Part of the relevant record has still not been made available even to the Senate.

IV

The Ratification Proceedings

THE ABM Treaty ratification proceedings are a bridge from the negotiating record into the record of subsequent practice. Although subsequent practice, and also the ratification record, should be a prior resort in interpreting the treaty, it follows logically from the negotiating record. Moreover, like the negotiating record, the ratification record strongly supports the traditional interpretation of the treaty.

The United States

Ratification hearings on the ABM Treaty were held before the Senate Armed Services Committee and the Senate Foreign Relations Committee in June and July of 1972. Hearings were also held by the House Armed Services Committee and the House Foreign Affairs Committee. On August 3, 1972, the Senate gave its advice and consent to ratification of the treaty by a vote of 88–2. These hearings and related floor debate have been subjected to review by both Judge Sofaer and Senator Nunn.[1]

1. Senator Sam Nunn, "Interpretation of the ABM Treaty—Part One: The

The question now placed in issue by the attempt thirteen years after ratification of the treaty to reinterpret its meaning was not envisaged by anyone either supporting or opposing the treaty at the time and was therefore not addressed directly in the hearings. A number of statements made in the course of the hearings, however, bear on the issue. Some general statements were not precise on the point and therefore would not clearly rule out either the new, broad interpretation or the traditional, restrictive interpretation. Others were, however, unambiguously supportive of the traditional interpretation, and *none* of the statements asserts the broad interpretation. The traditional interpretation was unanimously held within the executive branch, including by *all* of the treaty negotiators.[2]

Secretary of State William Rogers noted, in the Letter of Submittal, that Article V(1) limits development and testing to "fixed, land-based ABM systems and components by prohibiting the development, testing or deployment of ABM systems or components which are sea-based, air-based, space-based, or mobile land-based." He also explicitly made clear, in contradiction to the premise of the broad interpretation, that Article II of the treaty defines ABM components functionally, and not restrictively.[3]

During the hearings the late Senator Henry M. Jackson (D-Washington) asked Dr. John S. Foster, Jr., director of defense research and engineering in the Department of Defense, to confirm the prohibition on development and testing of, for example, a

---

Senate Ratification Proceedings," March 11, 1987, reprinted in the *Congressional Record,* daily edition (March 11, 1987), pp. S2967–86 (hereafter cited in text and notes as Nunn, *Cong. Rec.,* March 11, 1987); and Office of the Legal Adviser, Department of State, "The ABM Treaty—Part II: Ratification Process," May 11, 1987, reprinted in the *Congressional Record,* daily edition (May 19, 1987), pp. S6663–91 (hereafter cited in text and notes as Sofaer, *Cong. Rec.,* May 19, 1987).

2. This discussion is, in part, drawn from my own testimony before a joint hearing of the Senate Foreign Relations and Judiciary Committees on March 11, 1987, at this writing not yet published.

3. *The ABM Treaty and Interim Agreement and Associated Protocol,* Message from the President of the United States, 92 Cong. 2 sess. (Government Printing Office, 1972), pp. ix, x.

laser ABM system applied "if it is sea based, air based, space based, or mobile land based," but not "if it is a fixed land-based ABM system." Jackson asked, "Am I not correct?" Dr. Foster replied, "That is right," and he went on to state that "one cannot deploy a fixed land-based laser ABM system," but that one "can develop and test up to the deployment phase of future ABM system components which are fixed and land based."[4]

General Bruce Palmer, Jr., acting chief of staff of the U.S. Army, made several general and imprecise statements concerning the limitation on development of ABM lasers, but then clarified his testimony to indicate that the Joint Chiefs of Staff had carefully considered, and understood and accepted, the restrictive interpretation. He stated: "On the question of the ABM, the facts are that when the negotiation started the only system actually under development, in any meaningful sense, was a fixed, land-based system. As the negotiations progressed and the position of each side became clear and each understood the other's objectives better, it came down to the point where to have agreement it appeared that—this is on the anti-ballistic missile side—this had to be confined to the fixed, land-based system. The Chiefs were consulted. I would have to go to a closed session to state precisely the place and time. They were consulted on the question of qualitative limits on the AB[M] side and agreed to the limits that you see in this treaty." General Palmer also commented that the chiefs had agreed to the treaty, based on "a concept that does not prohibit the development in the fixed, land-based ABM system. We can look at futuristic systems so long as they are fixed and land based." He concluded: "The Chiefs were aware of that and had agreed to that and that was a fundamental part of the final [ABM] agreement."[5]

Secretary of Defense Melvin R. Laird stated, in a prepared written response to a question from Senator Barry Goldwater (R-Arizona), that "space-based ABM systems are prohibited," citing

4. *Military Implications of the Treaty on the Limitations of Anti-Ballistic Missile Systems and the Interim Agreement on Limitation of Strategic Offensive Arms*, Hearing before the Senate Armed Services Committee, 92 Cong. 2 sess. (GPO, 1972), p. 275.

5. Ibid., p. 443.

the language of Article V(1) banning the development, testing, or deployment of ABM systems or components which are sea-based, air-based, space-based, or mobile land-based. He also explicitly noted that in contrast to the ban on development and testing of space-based and other ABM systems or components, "there are no restrictions on the development of lasers for fixed, land-based ABM systems."[6]

The record clearly reflects the judgment of the executive branch at the time that the traditional, restrictive interpretation of the ABM Treaty was *the* interpretation, the only interpretation, of the treaty as it was presented to the Senate for its advice and consent to ratification. Yet in his October 30, 1985, analysis of the ratification record, presented to the Senate in the November 1985 hearings, Sofaer omitted entirely the prepared reply on this matter submitted by Secretary Laird. In his later (June 1986) *Harvard Law Review* article, Sofaer conceded—though only in a footnote comment— that Laird's official Defense Department statement supports the traditional interpretation.[7] In his May 1987 report, Sofaer included this material, but ignored it in his analysis. Similarly, Sofaer in 1985 omitted key portions of Foster's testimony, and even attempted to disparage Foster's qualifications by stating that he had not been involved in "the drafting or negotiation of the Treaty," a point that is forcefully refuted by Senator Nunn. (Nunn, *Cong. Rec.*, March 11, 1987, p. S2978.) Finally, Sofaer distorted and suppressed key parts of General Palmer's testimony, as again demonstrated by Senator Nunn. (See Nunn, ibid.)

Sofaer similarly ignores or glosses over the evidence that in 1972 the Senate also understood and accepted the traditional interpretation. The main and clear indication of Senate recognition of the traditional interpretation was the line of questioning by key senators such as Jackson. Yet in his 1985 presentation and testimony, Sofaer first excluded and then misrepresented Senator Jackson's statements. As Senator Nunn points out, Sofaer omitted entirely Jackson's own statements, which went well beyond the small excerpt

6. Ibid., pp. 39–41.

7. Abraham D. Sofaer, "The ABM Treaty and the Strategic Defense Initiative," *Harvard Law Review*, vol. 99 (June 1986), p. 1982.

cited earlier and showed the senator's detailed and correct understanding of the treaty constraints on future systems. Then, having excluded this evidence, Sofaer testified, incorrectly, that "fairly
read, Senator Jackson's comments do not address future
systems."[8]

The most dramatic indication of the Senate's clear understanding
of the treaty provisions as traditionally interpreted is in the remarks
of several senators who opposed the constraints on future systems,
in particular on development of space systems. Senator James
Buckley (R-New York), one of the two senators who voted against
the ABM Treaty, did so *because* the treaty "would have the effect,
for example, of prohibiting the development and testing of a laser-
type system based in space. . . . The technological possibility has
been formally excluded by this agreement." (Cited in Nunn, ibid.,
p. S2979.) No senator or witness challenged Senator Buckley's
assertion of the restrictive interpretation. Although Senator Strom
Thurmond (R-South Carolina) finally voted for the treaty, he
objected that it prevented development and testing of the mobile
systems, and the deployment of future fixed land-based systems.
(See Nunn, ibid.)

Sofaer introduces into his discussion of the ratification record
some of his unfounded assertions about the negotiating record.
Thus he argues that "the Senate was not informed of the refusal of
Soviet negotiators to accept U.S. language" on Article V(1),
although the Soviets explicitly accepted the substance of the U.S.
position, in language that the U.S. delegation and government
accepted as preferable. Similarly, he states that "the transmittal
documents were devoid of material that would have reflected the
dispute between the Parties over the meaning of 'ABM systems
and components,' " whereas in fact there was no such "dispute,"
and differences had been resolved in the negotiation, in particular
in exchanges in January 1972 that were excluded from the materials
Sofaer provided to the Senate. And he claims that "the Senators

8. *Strategic Defense Initiative*, Hearings before the Subcommittee on Strategic
and Theater Nuclear Forces of the Senate Armed Services Committee, 99 Cong.
1 sess. (GPO, 1986), p. 170; discussed by Nunn, *Cong. Rec.*, March 11, 1987,
p. S2978.

who exhibited a strong interest in the issue of future devices were not informed of the persistent, principled opposition of the Soviet negotiators to the regulation of such devices'' (Sofaer, *Cong. Rec.,* May 19, 1987, p. S6669)—an unfounded characterization of the negotiating record, in which the Soviets both in fact and in their explicit statements eventually *accepted* the U.S. position "completely."

Sofaer's interpretation of the material concentrates on general and ambiguous statements in order to argue that the record was "inconsistent and inconclusive" on the issue. He also argues, from the *absence* of Senate reservations or specific statements in its reports advancing the traditional interpretation, that "no indication exists in the ratification record that the Senate as a whole placed any importance on adherence to the narrow interpretation as a predicate to its willingness to give advice and consent." This is a curiously irrelevant standard to apply to a question of treaty *interpretation*. So, too, is Sofaer's gratuitous speculation that "given the little attention paid it, the complexity of the issue, and the overwhelming popularity of the Treaty, no evidence exists that the Senate would have failed to approve either the 'broad' or 'narrow' interpretation." (Sofaer, ibid.)

The executive and the Senate ratified the ABM Treaty in 1972 as it stood, was explained, and accepted—on the basis of the traditional interpretation.

The Soviet Union

In the Soviet parliamentary ratification deliberation, on September 29, 1972, in the absence of Foreign Minister Andrei Gromyko, First Deputy Minister of Foreign Affairs Vasily V. Kuznetsov, "on behalf of the Soviet Government," gave the Presidium of the Supreme Soviet of the USSR the official Soviet government position on the ABM Treaty. He drew attention among other things to the fact that "the parties are obligated not to create and not to deploy sea, air, space, or mobile land-based antiballistic missile defense systems or components." He presented this constraint as a clear obligation of the treaty as a whole, thereby affirming the official Soviet government interpretation that the provision of Article V(1) dealing with creation (development and testing), as well as deployment, of any space-based ABM system or component was not curtailed or overridden by Agreed Interpretation D or any other provision. He did not specifically address the matter of future systems based on other physical principles.

Marshal Andrei Grechko, minister of defense, also testified before the Presidium of the Supreme Soviet. He stated that the ABM Treaty "does not place any limitations on the conduct of research and experimental work directed toward solution of the problems of defense of the country against nuclear-missile strikes." That broad statement essentially asserts what adherents of both the traditional, restrictive and the new, broad interpretations agree: the treaty does not prohibit research or laboratory experimentation short of developmental testing. Even if the term "experimental work" were construed as including system or component testing, in my view not a warranted reading, it would still be entirely compatible with permitted development and testing of fixed land-based systems and components. Contrary to allegations made by some proponents of the broad interpretation, Grechko did not assert that development and testing of new types of space-based, air-based, sea-based, or mobile land-based ABM systems or components were allowed. Indeed, he made no statement about such systems, nor about future systems based on other physical principles.

In the Soviet ratification hearings, including earlier committee hearings as publicly reported, no one else addressed any of these issues.[9]

9. The quotations above and further observations concerning the Soviet ratification hearings are taken from the lengthy account of the proceedings published in *Pravda,* entitled "An Important Contribution to Strengthening Peace and Security," September 30, 1972. Kuznetsov had made a similar statement in a joint meeting of the Foreign Affairs Commissions (committees) of the two houses of the Supreme Soviet on August 23 ("In the Interests of Peace and International Security," *Pravda,* and *Izvestiya,* August 24, 1972). Grechko did not address that meeting, but his senior deputy, Marshal Viktor Kulikov did; Kulikov did not address research, or mobile, or future systems.

V

Subsequent Practice

SUBSEQUENT practice is the term used to cover the whole range of practical implementation of a treaty as evidence reflecting the understanding of the parties as to the meaning of its terms. It covers actions and statements.[1]

U.S. and Soviet Actions

The United States and the Soviet Union have without exception acted in accordance with the traditional interpretation. No Soviet action has even been alleged, by the United States or anyone else,

---

1. As of this writing, Judge Sofaer has not presented a report on subsequent practice to the Senate or the public. Senator Nunn has made a report: "Interpretation of the ABM Treaty—Part Two: Subsequent Practice under the ABM Treaty," March 12, 1987, reprinted in the *Congressional Record*, daily edition, March 12, 1987, pp. S3090–95. (Hereafter cited in text and notes as Nunn, *Cong. Rec.*, March 12, 1987.) In this report, Nunn notes and refutes earlier statements by Sofaer, who has admitted that his 1985 review of practice was deficient. See Don Oberdorfer, "Sofaer Disavows Portion of ABM Pact Stand," *Washington Post,* March 27, 1987.

to have gone beyond the traditional interpretation. The Reagan administration has charged the Soviet Union with one unequivocal violation of the ABM Treaty (the Krasnoyarsk radar), and several other actions possibly in violation or leading toward violation of that treaty, but none of these alleges any action concerning future systems contravening the traditional restrictive interpretation. The Reagan administration has also insisted that it is conducting its SDI program entirely within the constraints of the traditional interpretation.

Some skeptics argue that national means of verification may not be adequate to detect some activities going beyond the constraints imposed by the traditional interpretation, but that is a supposition and, whatever weight it may be given for other purposes, it does not lay adequate foundation for an argument on subsequent practice relevant to treaty interpretation.

Advocates of the reinterpretation argue that there has simply not yet been opportunity for testing advanced technologies. While that point does diminish the weight of the absence of contravening actions as an argument for the traditional interpretation, it does not provide a basis for arguing that subsequent practice lends any support to the reinterpretation.

U.S. Statements

Relevant statements are of two kinds: those between the treaty parties and unilateral statements reflecting interpretation of the treaty.

As early as the ratification proceedings, both parties paid close attention to statements of the other side. The U.S. record even includes senatorial comment on the presence of a Soviet Embassy observer at the open ABM Treaty hearing in 1972.[2] And the Soviet

2. *Military Implications of the Treaty on the Limitations of Anti-Ballistic Missile Systems and the Interim Agreement on Limitation of Strategic Offensive Arms,* Hearing before the Senate Armed Services Committee, 92 Cong. 2 sess. (Government Printing Office, 1972), p. 437.

side made no objection to or comment on the several unambiguous statements of the traditional interpretation reviewed earlier. Similarly, the United States had no objection to Soviet statements.

Judge Sofaer and Senator Nunn have both reviewed the record of U.S. statements made from 1972 to October 1985 that were relevant to the ABM Treaty reinterpretation issue. Sofaer argues that some statements were unclear and ambiguous. Nunn stresses that none supports the reinterpretation, and that while some were ambiguous, many others clearly stated the traditional interpretation. The congressionally mandated *Arms Control Impact Statements* did not address the point for the first three years of their existence, beginning in 1976 (fiscal year 1977); those for all years subsequent through 1985 (fiscal year 1986), including those submitted by the Reagan administration, explicitly stated the traditional interpretation: that mobile (including space-based) ABM systems, both current and future technologies, could not be tested or developed. (See Nunn, *Cong. Rec.,* March 12, 1987, p. S3092.) As even Sofaer acknowledges, the administration's SDI report to Congress in March 1985 "expressly embraced the restrictive interpretation." (Nunn, ibid.)

Over the years from 1972 through 1985 major analyses of the SALT agreements, including writings and statements by negotiators Smith, Rhinelander, Nitze, and me, set forth the traditional interpretation. (Again, for convenience, see Nunn, ibid., pp. S3092–93.)

While some other statements were less clear, *none* reflected the broad interpretation before McFarlane's statement of October 6, 1985. (See Nunn, ibid., pp. S3093–94.)

The Sofaer report on subsequent practice prepared in 1987 and pending release as this study goes to press reportedly may discuss at length various internal U.S. government and even nongovernmental papers and discussions from the late 1970s. While one cannot comment on these statements until they are publicly released, it should be borne in mind that they have no standing in international legal terms on the interpretation of the treaty and did not lead to any official change of interpretation.

Soviet Statements

Sofaer and Nunn have not dealt with Soviet statements since the 1972 ratification proceedings.[3] Sofaer has commented that the Soviets did not "begin explicitly to articulate the restrictive interpretation" until after the U.S. reinterpretation was announced in October 1985, and dismisses all Soviet assertions of it since that date on the grounds that they are merely opposing the American position.[4] His representation of the record before October 1985 is untrue; his dismissal of statements after that date is unwarranted. After all, one of the main arguments for the reinterpretation, particularly by Ambassador Nitze, was that the *Soviets* might not consider themselves bound by the traditional interpretation, and that the United States should not let itself be bound unilaterally. As Sofaer argues the point in his May 1987 report, "The ambiguity of the Treaty language, and of the negotiating record, would effectively have prevented the President from enforcing the narrow interpretation against the Soviets had they decided it was in their interests to support the broad interpretation." (Sofaer, *Cong. Rec.*, May 19, 1987, p. S6639.) While admitting indirectly that the Soviets had *not* adopted the broad interpretation, he ignores the fact that the hypothetical danger he conjures up could have been disposed of by obtaining a clear Soviet commitment now to the traditional interpretation.

Secretary Weinberger has gone even farther. He asserts that the Soviets do *not* hold the traditional interpretation. In a letter to Vice President George Bush as president of the Senate, also in May

3. The Congressional Research Service did promptly prepare a helpful report in 1985 addressed directly to the reinterpretation issue, at the request of the Senate Armed Services Committee, later made available for general congressional use. See Jeanette Voas, Office of Senior Specialists, *ABM Treaty Interpretation: The Soviet View*, 85-1020S (Washington, D.C.: Congressional Research Service, 1985), 18 pp.

Sofaer notes, and implies a broader meaning to, Grechko's 1972 statement to the Supreme Soviet earlier cited; Nunn refutes Sofaer's insinuation. (See Nunn, *Cong. Rec.*, March 12, 1987, p. S3094.)

4. Abraham D. Sofaer, "The ABM Treaty and the Strategic Defense Initiative," *Harvard Law Review*, vol. 99 (June 1986), p. 1985.

1987, Secretary Weinberger argued for application of the broad interpretation to the SDI program on the remarkable basis that a "critical ability of the Nation to investigate new technologies which hold the promise of a safer world will be seriously constrained by a *self-imposed interpretation of the ABM Treaty that is not shared by the Soviet Union.*" This statement is based on the specious attribution of a Soviet interpretation, as well as incorporating an unsubstantiated and incorrect assertion that the traditional interpretation is "self-imposed." [5]

Authoritative and insistent Soviet affirmations of the traditional interpretation since October 1985 are therefore quite relevant. And, as Nunn has noted, throughout the period from 1972 to October 1985, "the Soviets were on notice of U.S. adherence to the traditional view" and "made no objection." (Nunn, *Cong. Rec.,* March 12, 1987, p. S3094.) As I shall note, there have in fact also been clear and explicit Soviet statements of the traditional interpretation.

Some advocates of the reinterpretation go so far as to argue that all Soviet statements since March 23, 1983, are irrelevant, since they are made in opposition to the SDI launched by President Reagan's speech on that date. What such arguments conveniently overlook is that until then, there was no *need* for Soviet (or other) commentaries to address the matter, because there was no issue.

Of particular importance would be any statements of interpretation exchanged between the two sides, though the issue not having arisen, one would not expect to find many such statements, at least before 1983. There are at least two such exchanges that include significant and relevant Soviet statements. The first was between Viktor Karpov, one of the ABM Treaty negotiators, and his counterpart, Ambassador Ralph Earle II, during the SALT II negotiations. On March 16, 1976, when the question of the use of the word "currently" was in dispute, Karpov recalled that in negotiations on Article II of the ABM Treaty the word "currently" had been appropriate because that treaty was of unlimited duration and future components could emerge. In other words, he took for

5. Letter from Secretary of Defense Caspar Weinberger to the Honorable George Bush, President of the Senate, dated May 19, 1987, p. 2; emphasis added.

granted and espoused the traditional interpretation of Article II of the ABM Treaty.

Sofaer's assistants learned of Karpov's remark in 1985, but although William Sims, of Sofaer's staff, brought it to his attention, he chose to exclude it from his October 1985 report and his classified report of August 1986.

The second statement was by Lieutenant General Viktor Starodubov, then the Soviet member of the Standing Consultative Commission, to his counterpart, General Richard Ellis, in May 1985. He stated that under the treaty, ABM systems or components based on other physical principles could not be tested in space. This statement, which preceded the reinterpretation and was in accordance with the official American view at the time, clearly showed Soviet adherence to the traditional interpretation.

Numerous public Soviet statements from March 23, 1983, to October 6, 1985, were grounded in the traditional interpretation. Colonel General Nikolai Chervov, for example, the head of the General Staff directorate charged with arms control matters, including interpretation of existing agreements, objected in April 1983 that the Reagan SDI was "completely inconsistent" with the commitments of the ABM Treaty, in particular Article V(1), which he cited in full. He also specifically said that the treaty "bans both sides from developing antiballistic missile defense based on new physical principles—lasers, microwave radiation, beam weapons, and so forth."[6] A *Pravda* commentator noted that Article V banned development of space-based ABM components and challenged Reagan's declaration of acting within the treaty constraints.[7] Another Soviet analyst noted that the treaty created "strict constraints" on deployment of allowed ABM system elements, and that "it was prohibited to create, test and deploy *other forms and types* of ABM, sea, air, space or mobile land based."[8]

6. Col. Gen. Nikolai Chervov, Interview in *Bratislava Pravda*, April 29, 1983. He also noted that nuclear-pumped X-ray lasers in space would violate the 1963 Limited Nuclear Test Ban prohibiting nuclear explosions in space, the 1967 Space Treaty banning nuclear weapons and other weapons of mass destruction in space, and the 1980 agreement banning adverse environmental modification weapons.

7. L. Tolkunov, "Space Fraud," *Pravda,* May 10, 1983.

8. A. G. Arbatov, "Limitations of ABM Systems—Problems, Lessons,

Many Soviet accounts charged actual or prospective violations of the ABM Treaty by particular SDI tests. Thus, for example, several articles charged that a laser demonstration "strike" on a space shuttle was a "test" banned by the treaty.[9] This particular case is probably not a valid charge of a violation (I do not believe it was a test of an ABM "component"), but the relevant point here is not whether there was a question of compliance with the treaty, but that the Soviet *interpretation* of the treaty was the traditional one: that *testing* of ABM systems and components in space is banned. Many other examples of this kind reflect Soviet, as well as, at the time, American, understanding of the treaty in the traditional way.

One Soviet statement made before the Reagan administration's adoption of the reinterpretation deserves particular attention. On June 4, 1985, four months before Sofaer blessed the reinterpretation and McFarlane spoke, Marshal Sergei Akhromeyev, chief of the general staff and first deputy minister of defense, published an authoritative article on the ABM Treaty in *Pravda* in which he stated that Articles I, III, and V were "fundamental" to the ABM limitations. His elaboration of the traditional interpretation is crystal clear, even if his rhetoric is charged and some of his statements (such as research being prohibited) are unjustified.

> The ABM Treaty (Article V) forbids the creation and testing of space-based ABM systems or components, that is, precisely the objective of the U.S. "harmless research." In practice the creation of specific models of strike space weapons and even the testing of some of them are in full swing in the United States. Lasers of various types, electromagnetic guns, interceptor missiles, and antisatellite systems are being developed in laboratories and at proving grounds. All this so-called "research work" is in contravention of the ABM Treaty. . . .
>
> The provisions of the Treaty apply to any systems intended, as defined in Article II of the Treaty, to counter strategic ballistic missiles or their elements in flight trajectory. Since the ABM

Prospects," *SShA: Ekonomika, politika, ideologiya* (The USA: Economics, Politics, Ideology), no. 12 (December 1984), p. 19; emphasis added.

9. See, for example, "Projected Tests," *Pravda,* May 25, 1985.

components being created within the framework of the "Strategic Defense Initiative" are intended for precisely this purpose, that is, are designed to replace the interceptor missiles mentioned in the Treaty, all the provisions of the Treaty fully apply to them, above all the ban on the creation, testing, and deployment of space-based ABM systems or components.

The American authors of the "Star Wars" program are particularly zealous in propagandizing the thesis that the development of "exotic" anti-ballistic missile systems (laser and beam weapons, and so forth) is not only not forbidden by the ABM Treaty, but is even virtually encouraged by it. Thus P. Nitze, adviser to the president and the secretary of state on the Geneva talks, openly presents the creation of space-based ABM components based on other physical principles as an action permitted by the ABM Treaty. For greater cogency references are made to the Agreed Statement accompanying the Treaty (E) [D] which says that in the event ABM systems based on other physical principles and containing components capable of substituting, in particular, for interceptor missiles are created in the future, specific limitation on such systems and their components would be subject to discussion and agreement between the sides.

On the face of it this is a clear juggling of the facts. The aforementioned Agreed Statement regarding the Treaty indeed does not rule out the possibility of the sides' acquiring anti-ballistic missile systems "based on other physical principles," but only within the framework of the limitations envisaged by the Treaty as a whole, in other words in the single authorized area. The large-scale ABM system with space-based elements that the United States is planning cannot be restricted to a single area. It is a territorial and even a global ABM system that is totally prohibited by the Treaty. Therefore, the creation of laser, beam, and other such destructive components for that system is a direct violation of the Treaty.

Having embarked on a path leading to the destruction of the ABM Treaty, the U.S. leaders are trying to exploit the fact that the Treaty itself envisages in principle the introduction of appropriate amendments to its text (Article XIV). Therefore, they are saying that the U.S. actions running counter to the Treaty can somehow be legitimized, for instance, by revising this document and making amendments to it agreed with the Soviet side. They are making out that the Soviet Union too is no less interested in such amendments.

All this is merely an unworthy ploy aimed at reassuring public opinion. The U.S. side is well aware that by its actions it is not working toward making some additional clarifications to the sides' actions in the situations envisaged by the Treaty, which in fact, is what Article XIV refers to. The United States is working toward changing the meaning of the Treaty itself and emasculating it of its main content—the ban on the deployment of an ABM defense of the territory of the country.[10]

Having always held to the traditional interpretation, the Soviet reaction to the Reagan administration's adoption of the new, broad interpretation—prefigured in Marshal Akhromeyev's perceptive prediction—should have come as no surprise to anyone. The Soviet Union replied promptly to the White House reinterpretation.

10. Marshal S. Akhromeyev, "The ABM Treaty—An Obstacle in the Path of the Strategic Arms Race," *Pravda,* June 4, 1985. Incidentally, as his discussion makes clear, though not explicit, in the Soviet view Article I banning defense of the territory of the two countries prohibits space-based ABM systems.

Marshal Akhromeyev's attribution of the broad reinterpretation to Nitze and the administration was premature. In fact, in a speech made as recently as May 30, 1985, Nitze had reaffirmed the traditional interpretation explicitly (see Paul H. Nitze, "SDI and the ABM Treaty," U.S. Department of State, Current Policy 711, 1985, pp. 1, 3). Almost certainly what Akhromeyev's staff had misinterpreted (but with coincidental uncanny premonition) was the reference to an anonymous source in the administration as the author of the Heritage Foundation backgrounder of April 4, 1985, which did advance a version of the new, broad interpretation just two months before Akhromeyev's statement. This explanation is confirmed by the fact that Akhromeyev used the obsolete designation Agreed Statement "E" in his reference (I have indicated "D" in brackets in his text for clarification). The designation E was changed to D by the U.S. government in 1980 (for reasons unrelated to the interpretation question). But Harris had developed his interpretation in 1977 when the term used was E, and the April 1985 Heritage backgrounder continued to refer to E. Hence Akhromeyev's use also of E.

As indicated in the text following, by October 1985 Akhromeyev—and other Soviet commentators since that time—have followed the American lead and now refer to Agreed Statement D.

Again, Marshal Akhromeyev was chosen to set forth the official Soviet position in a major article in *Pravda,* on October 19, 1985. As it is authoritative and constitutes the most complete Soviet statement on the interpretation issue, the relevant passage is given below in full:

> A "new interpretation" of the treaty has been offered, according to which it purportedly allows the development, testing, and creation of anti-ballistic missile weapon systems on the basis of "other physical principles," that is, laser, particle-beam, and other types of weaponry, both land- and space-based.
>
> Thus, the presidential assistant for national security affairs, R. McFarlane, when appearing on an NBC television program on October 6, distorted the essence of the ABM Treaty. Trying to substantiate the "legitimacy of experiments" within the framework of the ill-famed "Strategic Defense Initiative," he contended that the treaty "sanctions tests of any ABM system as long as they are based on other physical principles." The ABM Treaty is also falsified by the "new confidential study" prepared by the Pentagon concerning limitations envisaged by the treaty. It is contended in the study that provisions of the treaty supposedly can be applied only to ABM radars and interceptor missiles, but not to the development and testing of "exotic" ABM systems (lasers, beam weapons).
>
> Such "interpretations" of the ABM Treaty, to put it mildly, are deliberate deceit. They contradict reality. Article V of the treaty absolutely unambiguously bans the development, testing, and deployment of ABM systems or components of space or mobile land basing, moreover regardless of whether these systems are based on existing or "future" technologies.
>
> In accordance with Agreed Statement D appended to the treaty, to which the administration now refers so often, the conduct of research, development, and testing of ABM systems or their components, based on other physical principles, is allowed in areas that are strictly limited by the treaty, clearly defined by it and using only fixed land-based ABM systems (as they are defined in Article III of the treaty). Moreover, if either side wants to deploy its new systems in these limited areas, it

cannot do so without preliminary consultations with the other side and appropriate agreed amendments to the treaty.

Only such and no other interpretation of the key provisions of the ABM Treaty, which were initiated by the United States itself, was worked out and adopted by the two sides in the course of talks on this treaty. The present aim of the U.S. administration is clear: to prepare a "legal base" for carrying out all stages of practical work within the framework of the SDI program, that is, the development, testing, and deployment of space strike systems.[11]

It is not necessary to cite all the numerous other Soviet discussions since October 1985 that reaffirm the traditional interpretation and reject the broad interpretation advanced by the Reagan administration. They include statements by the then Soviet defense minister, Marshal Sergei Sokolov, who added that the restriction of Agreed Statement D to fixed land-based systems "is confirmed by those officials who participated directly in the working out of the ABM Treaty"; an analysis in the principal legal periodical *Soviet State and Law*; and articles by several responsible Soviet officials involved in negotiating the ABM Treaty, including the chief of the Soviet delegation, Ambassador Vladimir Semenov, the current disarmament chief, Ambassador Viktor Karpov, and the former senior deputy foreign minister, Ambassador Georgy Kornienko.[12]

11. Marshal S. Akhromeyev, "Washington's Assertions and the Real Facts," *Pravda,* October 19, 1985. There had been a brief initial objection by TASS on October 9, 1985.

12. Marshal S. Sokolov, "Preserve That Which Has Been Achieved in the Field of Limiting Strategic Arms," *Pravda,* November 6, 1985; A. Natal'in, "The Illegality of the U.S. 'Strategic Defense Initiative,' " *Sovetskoye gosudarstvo i pravo* (Soviet State and Law), no. 11 (November 1985), pp. 113–19 (written in fact before the official U.S. reinterpretation in October, although not published until after it); V. Semenov, "The ABM Treaty and SDI," *Pravda,* February 21, 1987, first ed. only; V. Semenov and [Major General] B. Surikov, "The ABM Treaty—An Obstacle to 'Star Wars,' " *Mezhdunarodnaya zhizn* (International Affairs), no. 7 (July 1987), pp. 20–29 (General Boris Surikov had been a military adviser in the SALT negotiations); V. Karpov, "A Difficult 'Anniversary' " [fifteen years from signature of the ABM Treaty], *Pravda,* May 26, 1987, and "A Formula for Success—Europe without Rockets," *Novoye vremya* (New Times),

Inasmuch as Sofaer has not at this writing submitted his report on subsequent practice, it is not known how he will treat these and other statements confirming Soviet adherence to the traditional interpretation. According to some reports, he may argue that the whole Soviet effort in recent years to get a new agreement banning "space strike weapons" *implies* that the Soviet do not believe that the ABM Treaty bans such weapons. Such an inferential approach characterizes his treatment of the U.S. record with respect to the meaning and negotiation of the treaty. It would be equally challengeable in the case of determining Soviet views. But beyond that, and even beyond the clear and consistent record of Soviet adherence to the traditional treaty interpretation, is the fact that the Soviet definition of space-strike weapons is comprehensive. While it would embrace ABM systems and components, it also is explicitly directed at other systems not dealt with in the ABM Treaty, in particular antisatellite weapons and weapons directed from space at targets on earth. Space-strike weapons simply cannot be equated with ABM systems. Moreover, if the Soviet space-strike proposal duplicates or supersedes the ABM Treaty ban on space-based ABM systems, that does not imply anything that would at present diminish the ABM Treaty. By analogy, both the Soviet Union and, until 1982, the United States have sought a comprehensive nuclear test ban. No one has ever contended that their interest in such a treaty implied that they did not believe some categories of nuclear testing were already banned by the existing 1963 Limited Test Ban Treaty. Yet that would be the implication if the Sofaer approach were applied.

The Soviet subsequent practice from 1972 to date, like that of the United States from 1972 until 1985, has fully supported the validity of the traditional interpretation, and in no way the reinterpretation.

---

no. 17 (April 24, 1987), pp. 6–7; G. Kornienko, "A Look to the Past for the Sake of the Future," *Novoye vremya,* no. 21 (May 22, 1987), pp. 3–4, and under the pseudonym "K. Georgiyev," "Against Facts and Logic," *Pravda,* October 18, 1986.

VI

Problems of Interpretation and Compliance

IT IS AN obligation of parties to a treaty to consult and seek resolution of any questions that may arise as to their obligations. While there is no single established procedure, the duty to seek clarification of ambiguities and resolve differences of interpretation is clear. The matter may of course be submitted to some third party for arbitration or adjudication, but ordinarily a question of interpretation would be dealt with by the parties themselves.

In the case of the ABM Treaty, as noted earlier, there exists a body in which the two parties could seek to consult and work out any problem, the Standing Consultative Commission (SCC), set up in December 1972 pursuant to the ABM Treaty itself. Both parties, in particular the United States, have used the SCC to raise matters of ambiguity as to obligations under the ABM Treaty. For example, after extensive consideration, the two countries agreed on November 1, 1978, on an Agreed Statement on the application of the criterion in Article VI of a component "tested in an ABM mode." And as recently as July 6, 1985, under the Reagan administration, agreement was reached on a Common Understanding banning concurrent operation of air defense and ABM components

89

at ABM test ranges. The SCC is not, of course, an independent body; it comprises representatives of the governments of the United States and the Soviet Union. Use of the SCC is one appropriate way to resolve differences in interpretation, but there is no obligation for the parties to use the SCC; any other diplomatic channel could be used—embassies, emissaries, or arms-negotiating delegations. What does exist is the obligation to consult and not unilaterally to reinterpret a bilateral treaty, above all when the subject matter would alter in a material way the basic provisions and purpose of the treaty.

This problem of consultation has been compounded not only by the Reagan administration's persistent unilateral handling of the matter and refusal to consult and discuss it with the Soviet Union, but also by the unconscious double standard it has applied. This was brought out strikingly by a remark by President Reagan in his broadcast report to the American people on the outcome of the Reykjavik summit meeting in 1986. Referring to General Secretary Mikhail Gorbachev's proposal to strengthen the ABM Treaty by agreeing to ban all testing of weapons in space, Reagan no doubt in genuine innocence proudly declared: "What Mr. Gorbachev was demanding at Reykjavik was that the United States agree to a new version of a 14-year-old ABM treaty. . . . I told him we don't make those kinds of deals in the United States."[1] Irrespective of the merits of the Soviet proposal or the U.S. rejection, it was a proposal that the two countries *jointly* agree to a modification of the treaty to strengthen it. The "kind of deal" that the Reagan administration *did* make, less than a year before, was to try *unilaterally* to create a new version of the treaty weakening what had been jointly agreed upon and implemented for thirteen years.

Interpreting the ABM Treaty: Impact of the Reinterpretation

Any treaty is subject to interpretation and to possible divergencies in interpretation. The ABM Treaty has had relatively few

1. "Meeting with Soviet General Secretary Gorbachev in Reykjavik, Iceland," Address to the Nation, October 13, 1986, *Weekly Compilation of Presidential Documents,* vol. 22 (October 20, 1986), p. 1378.

problems in its fifteen years in force. Nonetheless, a few questions of interpretation have arisen, and others of likely future concern have been identified. Most have related to concrete applications of agreed constraints, such as defining activities covered by the ban on testing non-ABM components in an ABM mode. The SDI raised more serious questions of future application such as the precise meaning of "develop," "test," and "component."[2]

During 1983–86 many Soviet statements opposing the SDI program stretched the prohibition against development in Article V(1) to include research, but neither the language nor the negotiating history of the treaty justifies such an interpretation. While there remains a question of definition of "development," it clearly does not include research or laboratory experimentation. Since the fall of 1986, Soviet representatives and commentators have recognized and accepted the legitimacy of research, although a difference of interpretation remains.

Another significant issue concerns the meaning of the word "component" in terms of the constraints on development and testing in Article V(1). Once it is recognized that research and some testing is allowed, even in space, the problem is to define in practice what is permissible and what is not. Testing a laser sensor incapable of substituting for an ABM radar in an airplane or in space, for example, is permitted. The parties could also test a more powerful laser—for instance, one capable of striking the moon—as long as it could not strike a ballistic missile in flight. But a laser capable of striking and destroying a strategic ballistic missile flying through space would be prohibited, because it would be a potential ABM system component capable of performing the function of and substituting for an ABM interceptor missile. Clearly there are difficult questions of interpretation and potentially serious differences even if the traditional interpretation is reaffirmed by both parties.

The two most potentially important issues identified before the reinterpretation are not affected by it. One concerns antitactical

2. For a well-informed and useful commentary see Thomas K. Longstreth, John E. Pike, and John B. Rhinelander, *The Impact of U.S. and Soviet Ballistic Missile Defense Programs on the ABM Treaty* (Washington, D.C.: National Campaign to Save the ABM Treaty, 1985), 99 pp.

ballistic missile (ATBM) systems. The ABM Treaty, as stated in Article II, concerns "systems to counter *strategic* ballistic missiles"; systems to counter *tactical* ballistic missiles are not limited by the treaty, except in one respect. Any other system is constrained by Article VI, under which the parties have undertaken not to give missiles, launchers, or radars (including any in an ATBM system) "*capabilities* to counter strategic ballistic missiles or their elements in flight trajectory." The other issue is similar: an anti-satellite (ASAT) system that employed missiles, launchers, or radars would be similarly constrained.[3]

A third issue of interpretation relates to constraints on non-ABM radars—air defense radars, ballistic missile early-warning radars, and radars for space tracking and as national technical means of verification of strategic arms limitation agreements.

While these issues would not be affected by the ABM Treaty reinterpretation, some others would. The U.S. SDI program, for example, has drawn attention to the questions of interpretation of the terms "develop" and "components" in Article V(1) with respect to the ban on developing and testing new technologies. If Article V(1) did not apply to systems based on new physical principles, as the reinterpretation insists, there would be no need in the development and testing stage to define these terms because there would be no constraints on such activity. The same questions would, however, remain with respect to ABM systems and components based on "old physical principles," since they would still be banned under the broad interpretation.

A new question would also be raised by the reinterpretation: what are "new physical principles"? This question directly concerns kinetic-energy, or "kinetic-kill," technologies capable of hurling a projectile at super velocities, technologies of particular

3. Not all ASAT systems would be affected. The satellite interception system intermittently tested by the Soviet Union from 1968 to 1982 would not be, nor would the U.S. system under development since 1977, even though the latter employs interceptor missiles and an airborne launcher. Most systems using advanced technologies, such as laser beams for interception, would inherently have strategic ABM capabilities. For further discussion of the ASAT/ABM overlap, see Paul B. Stares, *Space and National Security* (Brookings, 1987), pp. 117–18, 145, 155–56, 166–67.

interest to those seeking an early deployment under the SDI. Is such a projectile an advanced form of "interceptor missile" or, like a disabling laser beam, is it based on new physical principles? At least some people in the present administration appear to have assumed it would be considered "new," although other observers, including Dr. Harold Brown, Senator Sam Nunn, John Rhinelander, and myself, argue it is not based on new physical principles. No attempt will be made here to do more than flag the issue as an illustration of the kinds of problems raised by the new reinterpretation.

In essence, the new, broad interpretation would threaten to render the treaty almost meaningless. It would raise the question of its consistency with Article I(2), which bans an ABM defense of the territory of the country. Even an SDI development and testing program based on the permissive interpretation could be construed to "provide a base for such a defense," which is banned. Moreover, the distinction between development activities and deployment would be blurred, and it is difficult to believe that the treaty could be maintained if testing of space-borne and other mobile ABM components and systems were unlimited.

Relation to Treaty Compliance and "Violation"

The reinterpretation poses a fundamental issue as to U.S. compliance with the ABM Treaty, particularly if it is ever put into effect as a permissive guideline for development and testing of space-based or other mobile ABM systems and components based on new physical principles. The SDI program itself, with the avowed aim of seeking to develop a system that could provide virtually complete ABM defense of the United States (and even its allies), poses the question of "anticipatory breach of contract." A program sanctioning unlimited testing and development of such a capability on the basis of a unilateral contested reinterpretation of the treaty would pose a profound question as to compliance with it.

The relationship between compliance and interpretation is often a difficult one. In some cases, a question of violation rests only on the facts of the given case: for example, is there or is there not an ABM radar some place other than where it is allowed by the treaty? Often, however, the fact of, say, the existence of a radar may not be in dispute, but rather its designation. And at this point questions of fact and of interpretation may be intertwined.

The Soviet Union does not dispute that a large phased-array radar is nearing completion at Abalakova, near Krasnoyarsk, in central Siberia. The United States believes, with good circumstantial evidence, that that radar is designed and intended at least primarily for ballistic missile early warning. Under Article VI(b) of the treaty, each party undertook "not to deploy in the future radars for early warning of strategic ballistic missile attack except at locations along the periphery of its national territory and oriented outward." The Krasnoyarsk radar is neither located along the periphery of the Soviet Union nor oriented outward. The Soviets argue, however, that the radar is not intended for early warning but for space tracking, and as such is not affected by Article VI(b) or any other part of the treaty, and in fact is explicitly exempt from a general large radar power constraint set forth in Agreed Statement F. This argument may not be persuasive to a skeptical and suspicious adversary, but even if it is unconvincing, it is difficult to refute. There is no guidance in the treaty or its negotiating history on how to determine that a radar is for space tracking and not early warning. (Nor, incidentally, if it is later used *both* for early warning and for space tracking, is there any specific guidance on how to deal with a dual-purpose radar with different constraints, although I would argue that the more restrictive constraint should apply.)

The United States has also built an early-warning radar, the new large phased-array radar at Thule, Greenland, and has planned another at Fylingsdales Moors in England. Neither is located along the periphery of the United States. The U.S. claim is that earlier non-phased-array early-warning radars at Thule and at Fylingsdales Moors were in existence when the treaty was signed, and that there are no constraints on "modernization." The Soviets charge that the radars existing in 1972 are allowed, but that their complete replacement by entirely new radars of a different type is not modernization, but deployment of new radars in violation of Article VI(b).

The Krasnoyarsk and Thule (and planned Fylingsdales) radars present problems of both fact and interpretation. In my judgment, both present serious questions of compliance.[4] The purpose here, however, is not to try to adjudicate these cases but to illustrate the intertwined problems of interpretation and compliance.

The Reagan administration's reinterpretation of constraints on developing and testing mobile ABM systems, if maintained and acted upon, would remove a common basis for judging compliance on a matter central to the viability of the ABM Treaty. It is clear that this consideration was not raised within the administration in October 1985, and indeed appears not yet to have been adequately recognized in the White House.

4. As the American negotiator of Article VI (with Nikolai Kishilov of the Soviet delegation), I am well aware of the negotiating record. Agreement on the provision was reached on September 8, 1971.

Incidentally, it was the United States that later (January 26, 1972) introduced the exceptions for radars for space tracking and national technical means of verification, agreed upon with little discussion.

VII

The ABM
Treaty Reinterpretation
and U.S. Policy

ULTIMATELY, the ABM Treaty reinterpretation is an issue not of treaty interpretation, or of the record of the negotiation and subsequent practice of the parties. It is a struggle between policy imperatives and the law of the land.

The ABM Treaty and the SDI

The new policy course set by President Ronald Reagan in his speech of March 23, 1983, led to the search for a loophole in the ABM Treaty that would facilitate pursuit of the Strategic Defense Initiative. The speech itself called for "free[ing] the world from the threat of nuclear war" through strategic ballistic missile defenses, although the president said the "long-term research and development program" he was launching would be undertaken "consistent with our obligations of the ABM Treaty."[1] Secretary Weinberger has stressed that "our goal is the defense of all our territory and

---

1. "National Security," Address to the Nation, March 23, 1983, *Weekly Compilation of Presidential Documents*, vol. 19 (March 28, 1983), p. 448.

that of our allies,"[2] although the ABM Treaty is based on the obligation of each party "*not* to deploy ABM systems for a defense of the territory of its country" (Article I) and "*not* to deploy [ABM systems] outside its national territory" (Article IX). Redefining those obligations is the easiest way to gain more leeway for the SDI, but if such redefinition comes to involve overriding the law of the land and the international treaty commitments of the United States, it is not acceptable as a matter of fundamental American policy.

The primacy of U.S. treaty commitments and American law should be accepted by all, regardless of views on the SDI. As Senator Nancy Landon Kassebaum (R-Kansas) has said, if the United States needs to pursue the SDI beyond the treaty limits, reinterpretation is "the wrong way to do it." Such an ardent advocate of the SDI as Senator Malcolm Wallop (R-Wyoming) argues that "questions of interpretation are a lawyer's exercise," that the fundamental question is whether the ABM Treaty remains valid "in terms of our own national security."[3]

Those who oppose the SDI as a matter of policy are certainly not likely to favor the reinterpretation. The harder case is for those who favor the SDI and would therefore wish to have the leeway provided by the reinterpretation. But, very much to their credit, some oppose the alluring shortcut of a unilateral reinterpretation on the basis of its lack of merit. Senator Sam Nunn (D-Georgia), a supporter of the SDI, is a prominent example. One of the ABM Treaty negotiators, Ambassador Sidney Graybeal, a strong supporter of the SDI research program, knows that the reinterpretation is not sustainable and has so testified before Congress.

Should the United States ever decide that its national security would be better served by freeing itself (and the Soviet Union) from the constraints of the ABM Treaty than by continuing to abide by them, it should withdraw from the treaty, or propose any amendment considered necessary and see if the Soviet Union

2. Caspar Weinberger, "We Need a Defense against Ballistic Missiles," Letter to the Editor, *New York Times*, February 10, 1987.

3. Both cited in David C. Morrison, "ABM Tightrope," *National Journal*, vol. 19 (July 4, 1987), p. 1752.

would agree, and if not then withdraw. The administration has not reached such a decision and in my judgment should not. But an unjustified unilateral reinterpretation is not an acceptable alternative or middle course.

The Reinterpretation and America's World Standing

The poorly coordinated consideration and casual introduction of the new interpretation by the U.S. administration in October 1985 compounded the distress of its allies and many other countries over earlier signs of American indifference to the outside world in taking decisions that affect their security and well-being. Not being consulted was bad enough, but it soon became clear that even within the administration there had been no real review either of the basis for the new position or of its consequences.

Confidence in the United States as a treaty partner, already buffeted by other experience, was further damaged. So was allied confidence in the U.S. leadership role in managing East-West relations. There was a growing inclination to see the United States as less interested, less reliable, and less successful in pursuing arms control than the Soviet Union under the new Gorbachev leadership. This concern was intensified by the obviously self-serving interest underlying the weakly supported American reinterpretation.

Most important of all, the action was subversive of the whole negotiation process, with the Soviet Union and generally. The most immediate and negative impact was on prospects for a new strategic arms limitation and reductions agreement. But the precedent itself was dangerous, and the broader effects difficult even to calculate. For example, future negotiations may be adversely affected by over-the-shoulder consideration of what a politically hostile later administration may use, out of context, from the negotiating record. There may be temptations to take out "insurance" by posturing or planting memoranda in the files for future disclosure if needed to protect a personal position or, conceivably, to sabotage a policy or a negotiation one opposes. The impact on negotiators of other countries (including, but not limited to, the Soviet Union) is yet another aspect of the fallout from efforts first to distort and then, by others, to correct the record.

Yet within the American debate, to say nothing of the situation within the administration itself, the international dimension of the reinterpretation has been little noted.

The Reinterpretation and the Executive-Legislative Relationship

Within the American political arena, there has been a tendency for the matter to drift into partisan confrontation. The administration has tried to make the SDI (and laterally the reinterpretation) into a kind of loyalty test, and has tried simultaneously to seek Republican support as a matter of party discipline and to seek Democratic and independent support (or at least less effective opposition) by claims of national security.

Experts have argued the merits of the case, and congressional hearings have sought to marshal the issues, but the question has seemed too technical and legalistic to attract much media and public interest, one way or the other.[4]

The reinterpretation has also raised a constitutional—and political—issue: the division of legislative and executive powers. The Senate, which the Democrats regained control of in the 1986 elections, has posed a question about its prerogatives in the ratification of treaties. How far can the president reinterpret a

4. Even in the Senate, by the time of new hearings in March 1987—seven months after the administration very reluctantly provided a segment of the classified negotiating history—only five of the one hundred senators had personally consulted the documents. Senator Carl Levin had been the first to present a report of his own study of the issue, including discussions with the treaty negotiators, before the documentary record had been made available, in December 1986. He was highly critical of the reinterpretation. Senators Joseph R. Biden Jr. (D-Delaware) and John Kerry (D-Massachusetts) have been active in investigating the matter and are also highly critical of the reinterpretation. Senator Nunn's extensive review has been most noted. Of those tending to support the reinterpretation, Senator Arlen Specter (R-Pennsylvania) has been an exception in interesting himself in the record and in interviewing negotiators.

treaty that has been ratified by and with the advice and consent of the Senate? If the substance of treaty obligations would be materially altered by a presidential reinterpretation, is the treaty the same as that to which the Senate consented? In the case of the ABM Treaty reinterpretation, the ratification record strongly supports the traditional interpretation. As Senator Nunn rather dramatically put it in February 1987, when the administration seemed intent on rushing forward with a decision to adopt the new interpretation in practice, doing so without extensive consultation with Congress would provoke "a constitutional confrontation of profound dimensions."[5] Senator Joseph R. Biden, Jr. (D-Delaware) has introduced a resolution that would reaffirm the legal relevance of the Senate's understanding of treaties at the time of its advice and consent to ratification, as well as reconfirming the traditional interpretation of the ABM Treaty. (Senators Carl Levin and Sam Nunn sponsored an amendment to the fiscal year 1988 defense authorization bill that would bar spending on development or testing of ABM components banned by the traditional interpretation unless Congress specifically concurred, but it does not raise directly the constitutional issue.)

Law, Politics, and Policy

The attempt to reinterpret the ABM Treaty began as a fresh hard look for loopholes that could legally be exploited in pursuing the SDI. When initial studies failed to find the desired leeway, attempts were made until a new "outside" lawyer found and embellished an approach to interpretation of the treaty that had originated, and been discredited, seven years earlier. This approach, with modifications, was espoused by Judge Sofaer, the new legal adviser in the Department of State. Sofaer approached the question with zeal as an advocate for the president's SDI policy. He was not impartial, nor did he see his duty as protecting the

5. Michael R. Gordon, "Reagan Is Warned by Senator Nunn over ABM Treaty," *New York Times,* February 7, 1987. The news account erroneously used the term "crisis" rather than "confrontation."

integrity of the legal position of the United States, or the legal and political foundation of the administration, or even the position of his immediate superior, the secretary of state. He evidently saw his task as conforming the ABM Treaty to serve the policy purpose of the president. The result was a serious distortion of the facts, a fatally flawed interpretation of the treaty, and a travesty of the law.

The Constitution of the United States charges the president to "take care that the laws be faithfully executed." And, in accordance with Article VI of the Constitution, the ABM Treaty is "the supreme law of the land." Questions of interpretation therefore require the most serious legal analysis, and not hasty, politically driven counsels of convenience.

To say that the ABM reinterpretation resembles the Iran-Contra dealings in a number of ways does not overstate the point. Both came to involve overzealous senior and middle-level officials of the administration ready to serve the policy desires of the president to the point of flouting the law of the land. Both relied on highly questionable, but never questioned, interpretations of the law. At precisely the same time that the ABM Treaty received its summary reinterpretation, September 1985, an inexperienced young attorney named as a political favor to be counsel of the Intelligence Oversight Board rendered a hasty, inadequate, and off-the-cuff judgment that the National Security Council (NSC) staff was not covered by the Boland Amendment, the congressional ban on U.S. military assistance to the Contras.[6]

Sofaer's opinion, registered in his memorandum of October 3, 1985, was not subjected to the slightest review before it was used as a basis for making administration policy. The reason is clear: it

6. Bretton G. Sciaroni had failed his bar examination four times in the District of Columbia and his native California before passing the examination in another state in order to be eligible to be waived into the $62,000 post at the IOB. He later admitted he had not consulted legal precedent, nor the key files on the issue, nor could he even explain why *he* had been asked to render the judgment. See Charles R. Babcock, "Cursory Review Led to NSC Opinion," *Washington Post,* June 9, 1987; and Fox Butterfield, "Key Contra Ruling Claimed by Novice," *New York Times,* June 9, 1987.

Sciaroni was also the anonymous government official credited by the Heritage Foundation for their April 1985 backgrounder that first publicly surfaced a version of the ABM Treaty reinterpretation!

gave a green light to those in the administration determined to go ahead. It gave them an authority to cite for a reinterpretation that would neutralize constraints of the ABM Treaty on the SDI program.

The circumvention and violation of the law in official U.S. government involvement in arranging military assistance to the Nicaraguan Contras and the contrived reinterpretation of the ABM Treaty both occurred because of a deterioration of governmental processes. The national security advisers—Robert McFarlane in both cases and John Poindexter in the Iran-Contra case—did not assure that the coordinating role of the National Security Council would serve the president. Indeed, Admiral Poindexter has testified that he did not obtain the president's approval or even inform him before deciding to divert Iran-scam funds illegally to the Contras, with all the consequences. When McFarlane took it upon himself to announce publicly the new ABM Treaty reinterpretation as a fait accompli apparently without obtaining the president's approval in advance, he prejudiced the decision and committed the administration to an unwarranted and unwise course.

Thus, not only was the legislative branch seen as an obstacle to be circumvented, but the executive branch itself was also intentionally fragmented and mostly cut out of the decision process so that it would not become an obstacle. The closest parallel is the Nixon White House in its last two years of travail. The main difference is that Watergate involved extralegal "plumbers" and attempts—in the main rebuffed—at illegal use of government agencies, including the CIA and the FBI, in internal political manipulations. In the Reagan administration's contra-vention of the law, the NSC staff and CIA coopted elements of the Departments of State and Justice; in the ABM reinterpretation, civilian Pentagon SDI activists coopted the Department of State's legal adviser. Lieutenant Colonel Oliver L. North testified that he would stand on his head if asked to do so by his commander in chief. Judge Sofaer has performed a similar act by standing the ABM Treaty on its head. But dedication to the desires of a president and the policies of an administration should never be permitted to exceed dedication to observing the law.

The initial legal reinterpretation of the ABM Treaty was sloppy, cursory, unprofessional, and unsubstantiated by the text or the negotiating record of the treaty. Once it had been prematurely seized upon and publicly pronounced as policy, it was beyond the pale for anyone in the government to question it. All subsequent efforts have been defensive moves to protect it and shore it up. It has never, within the executive branch, been subject to challenge.[7]

The internal lack of coordination reached a summit on October 6, 1985, when McFarlane announced the new U.S. policy position on national television apparently without even having discussed it with the president. From then on the administration's energies were directed to covering up the lack of preparation, coordination, and decision and to defending the position already taken, when necessary by withholding information that challenged that position.

The administration's commitment to the reinterpretation grew under constant pressure from Secretary Weinberger and Perle. In October 1985 Sofaer had conceded that the traditional interpretation was "plausible, but it is not the only reasonable reading."[8] By February 1987 Weinberger had gotten the whole senior administration team to refer to the reinterpretation as "*the* legally correct interpretation," and to deny legitimacy to the traditional interpretation.[9] And in Geneva, the American delegation was instructed to

7. In the brief period in September–October 1985 there were dissents and challenges from within the legal counsel of the State and Defense departments and the Arms Control and Disarmament Agency, but these were overridden and in some cases suppressed. Because of the haste and inexperience of Sofaer and his team, only a fraction of the relevant record was even located. One of those immediately involved has explained to me that those challenging the reinterpretation at the time relied too heavily on the September 1971 Article V(1) negotiation alone and were therefore caught short by the argument that Article II was also crucial. But when they located the key negotiations on Article II of December 20–21, 1971, this part of the record was to some extent distorted and to some extent suppressed. Much of the record was then not even consulted, once a "case" for the reinterpretation had been devised.

8. *ABM Treaty Interpretation Dispute,* Hearing before the Subcommittee on Arms Control, International Security and Science of the House Committee on Foreign Affairs, 99 Cong. 1 sess. (Government Printing Office, 1986), p. 13.

9. See Michael R. Gordon, "Arms and The Man's Language," *New York Times,* February 6, 1987; and R. Jeffrey Smith, "1972 ABM Treaty with Soviets

say that the United States accepted only the new, broad interpretation.

The various steps of American acceptance and insistence on the ABM Treaty reinterpretation were not part of an administration plan, although they were part of a strategy by Weinberger and Perle. The priority accorded to policy interest over the law was not deliberate, in the sense of any order or specific approval by President Reagan. But it also was not an aberration. The operating structure and pattern of decisionmaking of the Reagan administration not only permitted but encouraged initiatives in furtherance of policy that had the effect of circumventing or overriding the constraints of the law when the two were in conflict. It was understood, and understood correctly, by Casey and North that the president wanted continued military aid to the Contras, wanted the hostages released, and wanted a free hand for covert operations and the Reagan Doctrine—just as it was understood by Sofaer that the president wanted the SDI to be pursued vigorously and if possible in such a way that it could not be reversed; in the candid words of Attorney General Edwin Meese III, "so it will be in place and not tampered with by future administrations."[10]

The president did not ask anyone to violate the law, but he did not ask why the law seemed to become less of an obstacle than his advisers had predicted. And most important, at every level below, career officials and political appointees alike understood that findings that hindered desired policy moves were not welcome, while imaginative ways to circumvent legal obstacles were.

I have not served in the Reagan administration, but I did serve in the five preceding ones. While there have been ample precedents for many aspects of the covert Contra-aid operation, I do not believe the ABM Treaty reinterpretation could have become national policy in any of them. Some zealous official might well have come up with the idea, but there were always sufficient checks and balances within each administration (both procedural and in terms

Undergoes Fresh State Department Scrutiny," *Washington Post*, February 5, 1987.

10. "Meese Calls for Speedup in Deploying 1st Stage of 'Star Wars' Defense," *Washington Post*, January 15, 1987.

of the incumbents) that would have stopped the idea dead in its tracks.

The ABM reinterpretation, as well as the Iran-Contra scandal, were facilitated by, and also have further weakened, American institutions and political processes.

In seeking to place the matter in perspective, one could do worse than apply "the golden rule": what would the United States have thought if after many years the Soviet Union had suddenly, unilaterally, reinterpreted the ABM Treaty (or any other) to suit a policy purpose of its own contrary to U.S. policy and to the original clear understanding of both parties?

The Future: Where Do We Go from Here?

The ABM Treaty reinterpretation has placed the United States in a predicament, at least from the standpoint of all except those who wish to see the treaty and strategic arms negotiations collapse. The present administration is still divided on the question of whether to move to an actual application of the broad interpretation to its SDI program.[11] If it takes that step it will greatly intensify the issue both internationally and internally, and make later policy reversal still more difficult. But even if it does not take that further step, it is unlikely that this administration would repudiate the position it has already taken.

It would be appropriate and helpful if the Congress would enact legislation reinforcing the traditional interpretation and prohibiting the president from expending funds on testing activities that in

11. In 1985, Sofaer assumed the Reagan administration would *not* change its actual SDI program to allow application of the broad interpretation. In Senate testimony, in opposing a resolution that would require this administration to continue to act on the basis of the traditional interpretation, he argued "such legislation is unnecessary. The President has affirmed that he intends to pursue the SDI research program as currently structured, which is consistent with the 'restrictive' interpretation. Should a *future* Administration seek to implement the broader interpretation, the Congress would have a voice in that decision." (*Strategic Defense Initiative,* Hearing before the Subcommittee on Strategic and Theater Nuclear Forces of the Senate Armed Services Committee, 99 Cong. 1 sess. [GPO, 1986], p. 264.)

effect went beyond the constraints of the traditional interpretation of the ABM Treaty. The administration could not, however, be compelled to give up the new interpretation.[12]

A successor administration, with a different policy or a different attitude toward the law, could withdraw the reinterpretation. It could do so unilaterally or after reaching explicit agreement with the Soviet Union that both countries would abide by the traditional interpretation. Even if the Reagan administration adopts the broad interpretation in practice, a later administration could withdraw the reinterpretation, although probably at some political cost.

The United States could negotiate a common understanding of the interpretation issue with the Soviet Union at any time. If the present administration were prepared to do so, the routine five-year ABM Treaty review conference in the fall of 1987 would be an appropriate occasion. So would the ongoing Nuclear and Space Arms Talks in Geneva at any time. Ambassador Paul Nitze has publicly advocated doing so, noting, "It is hard to solve this problem unless one is prepared to talk about this."[13]

Beyond reestablishing the status quo ante October 1985, it would be desirable to work out with the Soviet Union the other questions of clarification and interpretation of the ABM Treaty.

Perhaps the best approach would be one under which the United States and the Soviet Union undertook to accept the traditional interpretation and to commit themselves to a continuing dialogue and negotiation in good faith on possible amendments to the treaty, either "tightening" it or "loosening" it (or both, in different respects), to accord with changing strategic and technological conditions. The ABM Treaty would be both the baseline for any change and a safety net against the disruptive and destabilizing effects of a unilateral action by either side. At the same time, it would explicitly acknowledge the need for joint consideration of changes either better to prevent, or to permit in a controlled way,

12. For an informed discussion of what Congress can do, see Lloyd N. Cutler, "Keeping the ABM Treaty Alive: What Congress Can Do," *Arms Control Today,* vol. 17 (April 1987), pp. 10–11.

13. "U.S. Arms Expert Asks Review of ABM Treaty," *New York Times,* June 20, 1987. Nitze had mistakenly believed his remarks were off the record.

ballistic missile development and deployment, but only by agreement.[14]

The reinterpretation of the ABM Treaty leaves a broad legacy, affecting not only the future of the treaty, the SDI, and strategic arms limitations and reductions, but also the development of U.S.-Soviet relations, America's world standing, and U.S. political life, above all the democratic tradition whereby policy accords with the rule of law. The United States cannot permit itself to be placed in the position of the village in Vietnam about which a U.S. Army captain sadly explained, "We had to destroy it to save it."

14. This approach is spelled out in some detail in an article addressed both to American and Soviet considerations; see Raymond L. Garthoff, "Refocusing the SDI Debate," *Bulletin of the Atomic Scientists,* vol. 43 (September 1987), pp. 44–50; and concurrently under the title "Security and Ballistic Missile Defense: Restructuring the Challenge," in *Mirovaya ekonomika i mezhdunarodnyye otnosheniya* (The World Economy and International Relations), no. 9 (Moscow, September 1987). See also Donald G. Gross, "Negotiated Treaty Amendment: The Solution to the ABM-SDI Treaty Conflict," *Harvard International Law Journal,* vol. 28 (Winter 1987), pp. 31–68, for a less far-reaching proposal for treaty amendment to deal with the current impasse.

The ABM Treaty

Treaty Between the United States of America
and the Union of Soviet Socialist Republics
on the Limitation of Anti-ballistic Missile Systems

The United States of America and the Union of Soviet Socialist Republics, hereinafter referred to as the Parties,

Proceeding from the premise that nuclear war would have devastating consequences for all mankind,

Considering that effective measures to limit anti-ballistic missile systems would be a substantial factor in curbing the race in strategic offensive arms and would lead to a decrease in the risk of outbreak of war involving nuclear weapons,

Proceeding from the premise that the limitation of anti-ballistic missile systems, as well as certain agreed measures with respect to the limitation of strategic offensive arms, would contribute to the creation of more favorable conditions for further negotiations on limiting strategic arms,

Mindful of their obligations under Article VI of the Treaty on the Non-Proliferation of Nuclear Weapons,

Declaring their intention to achieve at the earliest possible date the cessation of the nuclear arms race and to take effective measures toward reductions in strategic arms, nuclear disarmament, and general and complete disarmament,

Desiring to contribute to the relaxation of international tension and the strengthening of trust between States,

Have agreed as follows:

Article I

1. Each Party undertakes to limit anti-ballistic missile (ABM) systems and to adopt other measures in accordance with the provisions of this Treaty.

2. Each Party undertakes not to deploy ABM systems for a defense of the territory of its country and not to provide a base for such a defense, and not to deploy ABM systems for defense of an individual region except as provided for in Article III of this Treaty.

Article II

1. For the purposes of this Treaty an ABM system is a system to counter strategic ballistic missiles or their elements in flight trajectory, currently consisting of:

(a) ABM interceptor missiles, which are interceptor missiles constructed and deployed for an ABM role, or of a type tested in an ABM mode;

(b) ABM launchers, which are launchers constructed and deployed for launching ABM interceptor missiles; and

(c) ABM radars, which are radars constructed and deployed for an ABM role, or of a type tested in an ABM mode.

2. The ABM system components listed in paragraph 1 of this Article include those which are:

(a) operational;

(b) under construction;

(c) undergoing testing;

(d) undergoing overhaul, repair or conversion; or

(e) mothballed.

Article III

Each Party undertakes not to deploy ABM systems or their components except that:

(a) within one ABM system deployment area having a radius of one hundred and fifty kilometers and centered on the Party's national capital, a Party may deploy: (1) no more than one hundred ABM launchers and no more than one hundred ABM interceptor missiles at launch sites, and (2) ABM radars within no more than six ABM radar complexes, the area of each complex being circular and having a diameter of no more than three kilometers; and

(b) within one ABM system deployment area having a radius of one hundred and fifty kilometers and containing ICBM silo launchers, a Party may deploy: (1) no more than one hundred ABM launchers and no more than one hundred ABM interceptor missiles at launch sites, (2) two large phased- array ABM radars comparable in potential to corresponding ABM radars operational or under construction on the date of signature of the Treaty in an ABM system deployment area containing ICBM silo launchers, and (3) no more than eighteen ABM radars each having a potential less than the potential of the smaller of the above-mentioned two large phased-array ABM radars.

Article IV

The limitations provided for in Article III shall not apply to ABM systems or their components used for development or testing, and located within current or additionally agreed test ranges. Each Party may have no more than a total of fifteen ABM launchers at test ranges.

Article V

1. Each Party undertakes not to develop, test, or deploy ABM systems or components which are sea-based, air-based, space-based, or mobile land-based.

2. Each Party undertakes not to develop, test, or deploy ABM launchers for launching more than one ABM interceptor missile at a time from each launcher, nor to modify deployed launchers to provide them with such a capability, nor to develop, test, or deploy

automatic or semi-automatic or other similar systems for rapid reload of ABM launchers.

Article VI

To enhance assurance of the effectiveness of the limitations on ABM systems and their components provided by this Treaty, each Party undertakes:

(a) not to give missiles, launchers, or radars, other than ABM interceptor missiles, ABM launchers, or ABM radars, capabilities to counter strategic ballistic missiles or their elements in flight trajectory, and not to test them in an ABM mode; and

(b) not to deploy in the future radars for early warning of strategic ballistic missile attack except at locations along the periphery of its national territory and oriented outward.

Article VII

Subject to the provisions of this Treaty, modernization and replacement of ABM systems or their components may be carried out.

Article VIII

ABM systems or their components in excess of the numbers or outside the areas specified in this Treaty, as well as ABM systems or their components prohibited by this Treaty, shall be destroyed or dismantled under agreed procedures within the shortest possible agreed period of time.

Article IX

To assure the viability and effectiveness of this Treaty, each Party undertakes not to transfer to other States, and not to deploy outside its national territory, ABM systems or their components limited by this Treaty.

Article X

Each Party undertakes not to assume any international obligations which would conflict with this Treaty.

Article XI

The Parties undertake to continue active negotiations for limitations on strategic offensive arms.

Article XII

1. For the purpose of providing assurance of compliance with the provisions of this Treaty, each Party shall use national technical means of verification at its disposal in a manner consistent with generally recognized principles of international law.

2. Each Party undertakes not to interfere with the national technical means of verification of the other Party operating in accordance with paragraph 1 of this Article.

3. Each Party undertakes not to use deliberate concealment measures which impede verification by national technical means of compliance with the provisions of this Treaty. This obligation shall not require changes in current construction, assembly, conversion, or overhaul practices.

Article XIII

1. To promote the objectives and implementation of the provisions of this Treaty, the Parties shall establish promptly a Standing Consultative Commission, within the framework of which they will:

(a) consider questions concerning compliance with the obligations assumed and related situations which may be considered ambiguous;

(b) provide on a voluntary basis such information as either Party considers necessary to assure confidence in compliance with the obligations assumed;

(c) consider questions involving unintended interference with national technical means of verification;

(d) consider possible changes in the strategic situation which have a bearing on the provisions of this Treaty;

(e) agree upon procedures and dates for destruction or dismantling of ABM systems or their components in cases provided for by the provisions of this Treaty;

(f) consider, as appropriate, possible proposals for further increasing the viability of this Treaty, including proposals for amendments in accordance with the provisions of this Treaty;

(g) consider, as appropriate, proposals for further measures aimed at limiting strategic arms.

2. The Parties through consultation shall establish, and may amend as appropriate, Regulations for the Standing Consultative Commission governing procedures, composition and other relevant matters.

Article XIV

1. Each Party may propose amendments to this Treaty. Agreed amendments shall enter into force in accordance with the procedures governing the entry into force of this Treaty.

2. Five years after entry into force of this Treaty, and at five-year intervals thereafter, the Parties shall together conduct a review of this Treaty.

Article XV

1. This Treaty shall be of unlimited duration.

2. Each Party shall, in exercising its national sovereignty, have the right to withdraw from this Treaty if it decides that extraordinary events related to the subject matter of this Treaty have jeopardized its supreme interests. It shall give notice of its decision to the other Party six months prior to withdrawal from the Treaty. Such notice shall include a statement of the extraordinary events the notifying Party regards as having jeopardized its supreme interests.

Article XVI

1. This Treaty shall be subject to ratification in accordance with the constitutional procedures of each Party. The Treaty shall enter into force on the day of the exchange of instruments of ratification.

2. This Treaty shall be registered pursuant to Article 102 of the Charter of the United Nations.

Done at Moscow on May 26, 1972, in two copies, each in the English and Russian languages, both texts being equally authentic.

For the United States of America:

RICHARD NIXON
President of the United States of America.

For the Union of Soviet Socialist Republics:

L. I. BREZHNEV
General Secretary of the Central Committee of the CPSU.

Signed at Moscow, May 26, 1972.
Ratification advised by U.S. Senate, August 3, 1972.
Ratified by U.S. President, September 30, 1972.
Proclaimed by U.S. President, October 3, 1972.
Instruments of ratification exchanged, October 3, 1972.
Entered into force, October 3, 1972.

Agreed Statements

The texts of the statements set out below were agreed upon and initialed by the heads of the Delegations on May 26, 1972 [letter designations added later]:

[A]

The Parties understand that, in addition to the ABM radars which may be deployed in accordance with subparagraph (a) of Article III of the Treaty, those non-phased-array ABM radars operational on the date of signature of the Treaty within the ABM system deployment area for defense of the national capital may be retained.

[B]

The Parties understand that the potential (the product of mean emitted power in watts and antenna area in square meters) of the smaller of the two large phased-array ABM radars referred to in subparagraph (b) of Article III of the Treaty is considered for purposes of the Treaty to be three million.

[C]

The Parties understand that the center of the ABM system deployment area centered on the national capital and the center of the ABM system deployment area containing ICBM silo launchers for each Party shall be separated by no less than thirteen hundred kilometers.

[D]

In order to insure fulfillment of the obligation not to deploy ABM systems and their components except as provided in Article III of the Treaty, the Parties agree that in the event ABM systems based on other physical principles and including components capable of substituting for ABM interceptor missiles, ABM launchers, or ABM radars are created in the future, specific limitations on such systems and their components would be subject to discussion in accordance with Article XIII and agreement in accordance with Article XIV of the Treaty.

[E]

The Parties understand that Article V of the Treaty includes obligations not to develop, test or deploy ABM interceptor missiles for the delivery by each ABM interceptor missile of more than one independently guided warhead.

[F]

The Parties agree not to deploy phased-array radars having a potential (the product of mean emitted power in watts and antenna area in square meters) exceeding three million, except as provided for in Articles III, IV and VI of the Treaty, or except for the purposes of tracking objects in outer space or for use as national technical means of verification.

[G]

The Parties understand that Article IX of the Treaty includes the obligation of the US and the USSR not to provide to other States technical descriptions or blueprints specially worked out for the construction of ABM systems and their components limited by the Treaty.

Protocol

[A Protocol to the ABM Treaty was signed on July 3, 1974, ratified on March 19, 1976, and entered into force on May 24, 1976. This Protocol reduced the deployment areas allowed under Article III of the treaty from two to one, but did not change the treaty in any other way, and is not pertinent to the reinterpretation issue.]

Policy versus the Law
The Reinterpretation of the ABM Treaty
Raymond L. Garthoff

While congressional hearings on the Iran-Contra dealings have spot-lighted one case of conflict between perceived policy imperatives and the law, another has gone relatively unnoticed. Of no less importance in political, international diplomatic, and constitutional terms is the Reagan administration's attempt to reinterpret the Antiballistic Missile Treaty to allow more leeway for its Strategic Defense Initiative (SDI). This reinter-pretation poses a comparable issue of policy versus the law.

Signed and ratified in 1972, the ABM Treaty bans the development and testing, as well as deployment, of space-based and other mobile ABM systems or essential components. The administration, citing the treaty itself and the record of its negotiation, has claimed that the ban does not apply to systems based on new technologies.

Raymond Garthoff, one of the principal negotiators of the ABM Treaty, refutes that reinterpretation. Garthoff, who personally negotiated key provisions involved in this controversy, reviews the record point by point to demonstrate that the administration's view is unsubstantiated. He also shows that the ABM Treaty reinterpretation raises profound questions about the functioning of American political and governmental decisionmaking and about compliance with the law and adherence to international obligations.

Raymond L. Garthoff is a senior fellow in the Foreign Policy Studies program at Brookings. A career State Department officer, he was exec-utive officer and senior advisor at the Strategic Arms Limitation Talks (SALT) from 1969 to 1973 and U.S. Ambassador to Bulgaria from 1977 to 1979. Garthoff is the author of *Détente and Confrontation: American-Soviet Relations from Nixon to Reagan* (Brookings, 1985).

The Brookings Institution
Washington, D.C.

ISBN 0-8157-3049-7